WILD PIG

IN AUSTRALIA

By the same author:

Pack and Rifle
Hunter by Profession
Backblocks
The Deer Hunters
Fawn
Seasons of a Hunter
The Hunting Breed
Stag
Outdoors in Australia
On Target
White Patch
The Golden Years of Hunting in New Zealand
The Golden Years of Fishing in New Zealand
Razorback
The Wild Pig in New Zealand
New Zealand: Hunter's Paradise
Holden on Hunting
The Deerstalkers
A Guide to Hunting in New Zealand
The Hunting Experience
Hunt South
Wild Game
More Holden on Hunting
Fall Muster
On the Routeburn Track
Along the Dingo Fence
In Search of the Wild Pig
Station Country
Crocodile (the Australian story)

WILD PIG

IN AUSTRALIA

Philip Holden

Kangaroo Press

For survivors, wherever, whenever

Acknowledgments

That this particular project was a joy to work on can in a large measure be put down to the co-operation and, indeed, enthusiasm of the following people, and I should like to thank with utmost sincerity:

In Queensland—John McManus, Brett McCahon, Jim Mitchell, Graham Hardwicke, Jim Thompson, Joe and Nancy Geiger, Jerry Stanley, Tony Grasso, Laurie Porter, Joan Bentrupper Baumer, Brent Vincent, and Ron Teece.

In the Northern Territory—Ken Sheriden, Owen Rummings, Graeme Sawyer, Peter Caley, Greg Meyer, Rebecca English, Brett Ottley, Greg 'Hunter' Freney, Wayne 'Buffalo' Ross, Max and Philippa Davidson, Hans Fuchs, Geoff and Brett Crowhurst, John Downing for supplying contacts and Michael Clarke.

And in New South Wales—John McIlroy, Ron Mitchell, Mick and Debbie Williams, Gary Smith, Robert Nelson, Phillip Naughton, Russell Vivian, Robert Martin, Terry Korn, Ray and Sue Jones, Marty and Kellie Maxwell, Neil Teague, Richard Atkinson, Keith and Nora Roberts.

The author thanks Ray Jones for taking the two photographs of him in the Macquarie Marshes; all other illustrations are by the author.

Front cover: The wild pig, *Sus scrofa.*

Back cover: Success for Marty Maxwell and his eager assistants at Woollerbilla station.

© Philip Holden

First published in 1994 by Kangaroo Press Ltd
3 Whitehall Road Kenthurst NSW 2156
PO Box 6125 Dural Delivery Centre NSW 2158 Australia
Printed in Hong Kong by Colorcraft Ltd

ISBN 0 86417 629 5

Contents

The wild boar is not beautiful, but he is sublime in his lonely courage.

Philip Gilbert Hamerton, 1884

Introduction

In the early evening the two men came to a series of channel-like lagoons mostly fringed with pandanus palms. One man carried a rifle, the other a fishing rod.

Presently they disturbed a small saltwater crocodile which was stalking in a highly furtive manner presumably one of a number of plump burdekin ducks foraging at the water's rather murky edge. They also saw—and had seen for quite some time now—a great evidence of feral pigs: massive wallows that may have been used by generations of pigs, untold rootings, and wellworn pads like cattle trails leading away from water in all directions. Still, this was to be expected, a reason why they were here. In the dry season of 1993 an estimated 20 000 feral pigs enjoyed a rather sheltered lifestyle in Queensland's second largest national park.

The two men—John McManus and Brett McCahon—shared much in common. They were both in their early twenties, had a passion for hunting pigs, and both were employed by the Rural Lands Protection Board, operating out of Charters Towers. While Brett's work was mainly to do with weed control, John was specifically involved with feral pigs. And it was one of the Wet Tropics Management Agency's current pig projects that had brought them, as part of a five-strong team, to this part of Cape York Peninsula. Here in Lakefield National Park they were camped at Bizant Outstation.

Spearheading the team, and John's immediate boss at Charters Towers, was 40-year-old Jim Mitchell. Born on a Queensland pig stud, and pretty much tied up with pigs one way or another since then, Jim had worked extensively on pig control and/or research for a dozen years.

The third member of the group was yet another Queenslander: 42-year-old Graham Hardwicke. Based near Cairns, Graham had been with the department for eleven years. His work involved both weed control and the feral animal problem. Graham's area of responsibility was massive, extending from Cardwell to the tip of Cape York Peninsula, naturally including Lakefield National Park. Some of Graham's pig control work had taken him to the Channel Country, where pigs had long been rife.

A New South Welshman, Jim Thompson, 32, completed the party. Like Jim Mitchell, he too was a zoologist. In his own words, Jim worked out of head office in Brisbane and was directly responsible for policy and assessing pest animal populations in Queensland. Considering that Queensland's feral pigs number in the millions that was quite a responsibility.

For the record, this particular project in Lakefield National Park was concerned with an airdrop of about 5000 non-fatal, iodine-laced pig-baits of beef (feral cattle shot in the park) being spread over approximately 500 square kilometres of the park's overall landmass of 537 000 hectares.

Later, 200 or so pigs would be shot in what we might term stage-two of the project. This was to ascertain what percentage of the overall pig population should take the bait (the iodine content was revealed in blood samples) if large-scale poison drops were ever instigated here. Basically, it was all to do with the dreaded foot-and-mouth disease—an infectious viral disease of livestock—in case it ever infiltrated the far northern tropical regions and feral pigs then contracted it, which is by no means a certain outcome.

Meanwhile, Brett McCahon and John McManus continued their pleasant evening stroll along the almost linking network of lagoons in the watershed of the Bizant River. Basically, Lakefield National Park embraces the many deltas and intertwining channels of a number of rivers draining into Princess

Charlotte Bay: the Kennedy, Normandy, Hann, Morehead, and, of course, the Bizant. Geographically speaking, it is low-lying terrain prone to extensive flooding in the wet.

As the two men linked together and exchanged a few words, several pelicans lifted almost sluggishly from an isolated pool before them. Holding a department-issue .308 semi-automatic Heckler & Kock in the crook of his arm, John cast an eye over fresh pig rooting and expressed some surprise that they hadn't seen a pig.

'We saw a good 'un this morning, but,' said Brett with a big grin. True enough. They had. Early on, they had watched a black boar rooting in a swampy creek system. Because they were required to shoot a number of pigs to obtain pre-baiting blood samples (for a comparison with those that would later take the iodine-laced bait) they decided to shoot it. John had taken the shot. Just one.

It was an interesting boar—old now, with blackened tusks both thick and stunted. Across his back were the criss-crossed scars of battles with other boars—fights over females, over territory, and perhaps because they just fancied a darn good scrap. An aged warrior, then, whose number had come up one July morning. Using a rope and pulley system— over the limb of a tree—they had hauled the carcass off the ground and found that his live weight came to 113 kg.

Now, with a smile, Brett shook his fishing rod at his mate.

'Might do better with this, eh?'

'We might at that, too.' He grinned. No one back at camp was going to object to fresh barramundi for dinner tonight, now were they? 'Be a good idea to get another pig before that,' John went on, meaning they would hunt a little longer before Brett cast out a line in a likely spot. 'Besides it'll keep old Jim happy, won't it.'

A rather shallow stretch of water spread itself before them now, more like floodwaters than an actual lagoon. Both men noticed the deep rooting— indicating a large pig or pigs—at the water's edge. Now as John swung wide to avoid the water, Brett started through it, angling away from John to the far side.

Brett stooped under the branches of a tree, the water nearly up to his knees—deep enough, he realised with a start, to conceal a very large crocodile.

Suddenly there was a loud splashing sound behind Brett. Spinning around, fearing the worst, he was thunderstruck to see a large black boar hurtling towards him through the churning water; later, he would say that he had never seen anything move so quickly.

But despite the heart-stopping impact the sight of the charging boar had on him, Brett was still able to marshal his actions constructively: he hurled the fishing rod from him, grabbed a branch above his head and then like a gymnast swung himself off the ground and up into the interlocked limbs and out of harm's way.

Without breaking speed the boar altered course.

Brett saw the boar making a direct beeline for John, who was standing at the water's edge with his rifle to his shoulder. To Brett, holding his breath, John appeared as ice cold as a beer in a chiller. But the boar was almost upon him now and still John hadn't fired! My God, Brett thought, he's frozen, unable to act! A millisecond later the .308 roared.

Head-shot, the boar went down hard. It skidded on its side in the water like a suddenly capsized jetboat, stopping several paces from where John stood, ready to shoot again if need be, the brim of his battered Akubra, holed at the peak of the crown, slanting low over his eyes.

When Brett reached John, he slapped him hard on the shoulder, praising the great shot he had made. Grinning, John shrugged in a matter-of-fact manner and said that he really didn't have that much choice in the matter, now did he? They both laughed at that and John remarked in that rather low-key style of his that at least they had another blood sample now, didn't they? And that really broke Brett up.

They turned their attention to the boar—black as the Ace of Spades, in fine condition, and perhaps even heavier than the one John had shot this morning— 120 kg tops. Moreover, his tusks were formidable weapons. At close quarters, and given the opportunity to use them . . . well, that wasn't a sensible thought to dwell on.

John McManus and Brett McCahon were still in a heady state of near intoxication as they forgot all about fishing for barramundi and retraced their steps some distance to where they had parked a Toyota Landcruiser; talking constantly about what they had experienced they returned to Bizant Outstation in the dry season of 1993.

Above: Sus scrofa in a feral state.

Left: John McManus, Lakefield National Park

Above: Wild boar at bay

Below: Graham Hardwicke using a Sako .264 Magnum, ideal for open plains hunting.

Above left: Jim Mitchell.

Above right: Joe Geiger standing in front of the original homestead on Hammond Downs.

John McManus (*left*) and Brett McCahon with a 113 kg (live weight) boar.

The wild boar is equipped with formidable weapons.

The powerful snout of the adult wild boar.

Caught in the wild, the banded/general colouration of the piglet in the foreground is a direct throwback to the true wild boar.

1 Profile of a Species

The origin of all our domestic animals will probably remain forever vague.

Charles Darwin

Hammond Downs Station, On Cooper Creek, Southwest Queensland

As the first rays of the sun speared like dazzling bolts of orange-coloured light across the grassy plain a large black boar stood almost defiantly near a dry creekbed. The boar, backlit by the sun, and with hackles raised and ears erect, was facing a beat-up Toyota Landcruiser barrelling towards it over rock-hard corrugations that would in very little time shake a conventional family vehicle to bits.

Suddenly the boar whirled about—fast, like a spooked feral cat. Then off. Pellmell. With the majority of his considerable weight up front in those extraordinarily developed, slab-like forequarters, the boar's sudden turn of speed was nothing short of electrifying . . .

Hammond Downs station is near Windorah. Owned by Joe and Nancy Geiger, it is a pretty typical run in the outback where they periodically battle flood, bushfire, drought, or falling prices for either sheep or cattle with the same stoical determination not to give up—no matter the cost or the sacrifice— that pretty much characterised those people who first made a success of raising stock in Queensland's uncompromising hinterland.

When I paid the likeable Geigers a visit the previous day, Joe had said, yeah, there were plenty of pigs on their place, he knew just where they were, and would I like to see some? Well, there had been only one answer to that, right, and so here we were early next morning in hot pursuit of a large black boar hellbent on reaching a tree-fringed watercourse before we did.

Grinning like a big kid, Joe slammed his foot down hard on the accelerator. As we picked up speed and started to close the gap between boar and vehicle, the terribly uneven ground, often under several metres of water when the nearby Cooper floods, seemed to flatten out so that the Toyota went over, rather than into, a continual series of wave-like depressions.

With the engine screaming as though in protest against such inconsiderate treatment, we drew level with the outstretched animal. The boar was in full flight now—a magnificent, streamlined creature.

With a laugh, Joe pulled to a halt and the boar, glancing over its shoulder, slowed to a tail-swinging trot and started across the mostly dried-up watercourse.

Whichever way you wish to look at it, this was a most fortunate pig. Here in southwest Queensland pigs are about as popular as a mutton-loving wild dog on the wrong side of the Dingo Fence, and, while Joe always carries a high-power rifle with him in the cabin of the Toyota, then he does, as you've most likely gathered, have a rather soft spot for pigs and would only take severe control measures if and when it became absolutely essential for him to do so.

Presently we saw more pigs. They were wallowing near Cooper Creek. The clinging mud, that glistened like newly-mixed cement on their compact frames, would, before too long, be baked hard by a 40-degree sun.

Later, as we returned to the homestead, I reflected on the pigs I had seen today: they had seemed so entirely natural in their surroundings, so very much a part in the overall scheme of things, that it seemed impossible to believe that they were not native to this vast island continent.

The wild pigs of Australia belong to a family that is well represented in both the Old and New World. They are classified as Suidae—meaning Old World Pigs—and as such are the oldest and most primitive of all living even-toed ungulates.

Many millions of years ago wild pigs—of a more ancient derivative—ranged over much of Europe, Africa, and Asia. Pigs foraged in the vast forested country now buried forever under the Gobi Desert (nowadays too arid to sustain them). In the Silwalik Hills in India roamed a giant pig—*Sus giganteus*—which is thought to have stood as tall as a mule and is known to have had a skull that measured 60 centimetres. The fossil remains of pigs have been discovered alongside those of the extinct mammoth and mastodon in various parts of Asia and Europe, including England. Significantly, the pig we know today represents one of the most ancient gigantic mammalian forms.

The Suidea comprise five genera, the most familiar, and the one we are most concerned with, being the genus *Sus* (of Eurasian origin). Within this group we find the European wild boar (*Sus scrofa scrofa*), the Indian crested pig (*Sus scrofa cristatus*), the domestic pig (*Sus domestica*), and the feral pig (*Sus scrofa*). The word 'feral' indicates an animal that has reverted from domesticated stock to completely wild.

Precisely when man first domesticated the pig will always be unclear. It may well be that the pig—rather than the cat or dog—was the first animal man domesticated and as such that it figured prominently

in the migration of the human species.

Sir Arthur Keith believes that pigs were domesticated in Persia during the closing of the Ice Age, and cites positive evidence to substantiate this claim in the ancient city of Persepolis.

It appears that sheep and goats were the first animals to be 'farmed' by villagers in the Middle East, about 9000 BC. Pigs were added to the short list some 2000 years later. From the findings—that is, bone counts—of archaeologists at such early prehistoric farm sites they have deduced that the domesticated pig was invariably considered a minor part of the food chain, perhaps no more than 5 per cent. Given the geographical location of the Middle East—and that sheep and goats are much better suited than pigs to semi-arid conditions—then this is perhaps only to be expected; for, unlike sheep and goats, the pig has to be provided with both shade and mudholes, it cannot be milked, and it eats the same food as man.

Still in prehistorical times, pigs were domesticated in Switzerland, and in the neighbourhood of the Baltic Sea. A Chinese scholar has estimated that his people domesticated the pig about 2900 BC.

It has of course long been the practice of man to take his domestic animals with him when he settled new lands. Zoologists are of the opinion that the pig, dog, and fowl found in Polynesia all had their home in the Indo-Malayan region.

The original geographical distribution of the Indian crested pig or Eurasian wild boar is unclear. V.G. Heptner (1966) considers the species may have been present in the Philippines but had not extended its natural range to the lesser southeast Indonesian islands and the New Guinea regions. Expanding on this, Heptner goes on to say:

It is very difficult to work out the actual natural [original] area of distribution of the wild pigs in the very far south-eastern region and perhaps already impossible. This is so because the inhabitants of these areas, who were excellent sailors, brought already in early times the domestic pig with them when they colonized the island. These domestic pigs became wild and changed into genuine wild pigs. This is particularly true of New Guinea and the adjacent group of islands which are populated by *Sus scrofa papueuris*. However, wild pigs of other parts of the islands between Australia and Asia also have similar features to domestic pigs. Even the wild pigs on the Celebes Islands have these 'domestic' characteristics. Apparently interbreeding took place in some areas between genuine wild pigs to these areas and introduced pigs which became wild.

Heptner's words could serve as a blueprint for whenever and wherever wild and domestic pigs have intermingled.

In any event, these adventurous people gradually introduced the pig to virtually all of the main islands in the South Pacific. For instance, the pig was introduced to Fiji about 1300 BC. In New Guinea the remains of pigs estimated to be 6000 years old have been discovered, obviously indicating an introduction at, but most likely before, this date. In commenting further on this point, Simon E. Townsend writes:

> Since the Australian seas probably did not reach their present level till approximately five thousand years before the present, New Guinea and Australia may not have been separated by any significant water barrier 6000 years ago. Theoretically, it is possible that pigs might have entered Australia at a date much earlier than is yet substantiated. It is possible that some could be of Asian origin. Their ancestors may have been brought to the north of Australia by Asian travellers or fishermen within historical times. Archaeological evidence is lacking to support this, therefore the feral pig cannot authoritatively be said to have a history in Australia any longer than that of European settlement.

At any rate the pig in the South Pacific regions was—and still is today—used symbolically to express rank in both social and religious functions.

It is possible that the pig was used initially as a scavenger by all peoples before it was discovered how good its flesh was to eat. The early Egyptians, for instance, used pigs to clean up roots and dead fish along the banks of the Nile. But most certainly those same Egyptians, Romans and Greeks all soon realised the advantages of raising pigs for meat: they were comparitively easy to raise in captivity; could be fed virtually anything, and very little of the carcass was wasted.

During the period when the Egyptians did not eat pork and loathed pigs as unclean animals and even emblems of evil, they nonetheless did not dispense with their services but used them in the process of treading grain into tilled soil—that is, the pigs used their feet to work the seed from the surface into the ground, where it not only germinated but was also safe from birds. The Greek historian Herodotus, in his description of Egypt, wrote that pigs were commonly and universally employed to tread corn.

In the time of the Saxons, pigs were held in high esteem. An illustration in Queen Mary's Psalter (1310) depicts swineherds knocking acorns off oak trees for pigs to feed on; the pigs are shown as long in the leg, hairy, razor-backed. The wild boar, as we shall read, was still comparatively common in many parts of Great Britain then.

As a matter of interest, the European wild boar, and all pigs for that matter, loves nuts. Using its lips and teeth, as sensitive in this instance as are those of a female saltwater crocodile when handling its young or eggs, a pig has no difficulty in removing the shell of even the smallest nuts. It is very much as the poet, Bloomfield, wrote:

> From oak to oak they run with eager haste,
> And wrangling share the first delicious taste of fallen acorns.

The word swine—meaning pig and of Teutonic origin—occurs in many English places names, such as, for instance the eleventh century village of Swine in Holderness.

The position of swineherd in such villages was, as Ida Mellen tells us in *The Natural History of the Pig*, a most prestigious one:

> In olden times pigs were cared for by swineherds, the office of the swineherd in Gaul, Britain and other lands being a meticulous one, his duties multifarious. In the morning he assembled the pigs of his village by sounding a horn in England, a bagpipe in other places, or by using his voice were it powerful and then escorted his herds to their grazing grounds. At the end of the day they returned under his guidance. On entering the village each ran to its own sty, and it is said they never were known to make a mistake. It was his duty to spay the females and geld the males, to know every animal in the herd, its condition and health, each sow and her piglets, and also to clean the sties; for, as it was anciently observed, 'Though it wallows in the mire, it is very desirous of a clean lodging and delighteth of the same'.

In such close contact with pigs, swineherds became aware that like the cat their charges were extremely sensitive to changes in the weather. In uncanny anticipation of falling barometric pressure—that is, gale-force winds and low temperatures—they displayed extreme apprehension. Today, the pig is considered the most reliable and accurate of living barometers. Also, pigs have an acute sense of time: they know when the feeding hour has arrived, and even in cases where they were more loosely cared for and were perhaps fed but once a week then they would arrive collectively at the right place and at the correct hour.

There is a particularly lovely little story of a swineherd whose pigs were stolen by pirates. The swineherd waited until the pirates were rowing out of the port, and then rushing to the water's edge, he gave the call which his pigs recognised. Responding instantly the pigs flocked to one side of the boat and capsized it. Being fine swimmers the pigs made it safely ashore, much to the relief of their master, but as for the robbers, well, they were justly drowned.

Scientific breeding of pigs commenced in the eighteenth century when pigs from east and southeast Asia were brought to Europe and crossed with local pigs. However, the ancestors of the 300-plus domestic breeds we know today, and of course the far-ranging feral pig, are basically linked to just two wild species: the European wild boar and the Indian crested pig.

The European Wild Boar (*Sus scrofa scrofa*)

Certainly pigs were among the animals most familiar to primitive man of the Eastern Hemisphere. There is, for instance, a drawing of a European wild boar on the wall of the world-famous Altamira Cave in Spain dating back some 25 000 years.

The European wild boar was once common in Britain. Howard the Good, in the tenth century, allowed his grand huntsmen to 'chace' the wild boar from the middle of November through to the beginning of December, what might of course be termed an extremely limited hunting season.

William the Conqueror, who ascended to the throne of England in 1066, was a keen huntsman himself. The hunting of wild boar was of course a privilege reserved for royalty and noblemen and anyone who hunted the wild boar without permission and was convicted of such a crime was punished most severely by the loss of his eyes.

In 1124 a famous wild boar in Scotland, which had eluded hunters for a number of years and which was credited with killing many dogs, was at last put to rest. The mighty animal had tusks 30 centimetres in length.

When describing London in 1174, Fitz-Stephen says that the vast forest on the north side of the city was ' . . . the retreat of wild boars'.

Hunting the wild boar remained in favour with royalty, and both Henry IV, early in the fifteenth century, and James I in 1617 hunted near the royal castle at Windsor.

But by the time Charles I came to power in 1624, the once plentiful wild boar, due to a severe loss of habitat and large-scale poaching, was very much an endangered species over almost all of its range. The new monarch, with a view to reversing this deplorable situation, obtained wild boar from both Germany and France, where they were far from endangered. These boars were liberated in the New Forest in Hampshire.

J.E. Harting, in his 1880 publication *British Animals Extinct Within Historical Times,* says in regards to these 'imported' wild boars that they ' . . . encreased and became terrible to the travellers. In the cival warres they were destroyed but they had tainted all breeds of pigges of the neighbouring partes, which are of their colour; a kind of soot colour.' Pigs fitting this description were still being observed in the New Forest as late as 1791. It was also about this time that they were reintroduced to a forest in Essex, but as Harting put it, ' . . . they digged the earth so up, and did such spoyle, that the country would not endure it'.

The wild boar was considered extinct in Britain by the end of the seventeenth century. Later attempts to reintroduce the species into Great Britain—mainly to enclosed parks—failed. The wild boar, however, was successfully re-established in both Sweden and Norway, where it had become extinct for the same reasons as in Britain.

On at least four separate occasions—in the 1890s, 1910, 1912 and 1925—the European wild boar was introduced into the USA. The 1912 introduction is worth commenting on. An English sportsman, George Gordon Moore, imported fourteen pigs—mostly boars—and turned them into a 1500-acre (600-hectare) hunting reserve in the Appalachian Mountains of North Carolina. Initially, they were restricted to a special pen constructed of strong chestnut rails. At the time there was considerable speculation about how they would react to the comparatively small enclosure. They were of course wild animals and must have endured considerable indignities since being captured and transported by sea, train and, last of all, bullock-drawn wagon. We may presume the boars were heartily sick of being confined because, with awesome power, as befitting *Sus scrofa scrofa*, they attacked the fence and, to a pig, broke free. In total despair, George Gordon Moore watched them escape into the nearby forest. Soon, with typical pig audacity, the boars were mating at will with unpenned domestic stock and today an untold number of hybrid pigs inhabit some of the wildest terrain in North Carolina and Tennessee. Some of the boars grow to a prodigious size and are commonly referred to as the Russians; while this term indicates where Moore obtained his stock, it is more likely they came from Germany or Poland, either way your true-blue *Sus scrofa scrofa*.

During the early 1930s, a number of 'Bavarian' wild boar were imported into several exotic forests in the southwestern Cape of South Africa to control the larvae of the pine emperor moth, which was defoliating the trees. The basic idea was that the pigs would root out the moths' pupae, which, among other things, they most successfully did. As with wild boar introduced into North America, they gradually intermixed with domestic stock and today their descendants provide hunters with grand sport and local authorities with all sorts of unwanted problems.

Apart from man, the main enemy of the European boar—in its traditional range—is the wolf. They are implacable enemies. Traditionally, wolves hunt in packs and therein lies their advantage—they simply outnumber their prey. A German forest warden once told of how he was able, by the signs he found, to reconstruct the pattern of a battle between one boar and five wolves. The wolves, of course, won, for the forest warden found the boar dead. It must, he realised, have been an awesome battle, for there were five separate blood-stained tracks leading away from where the valiant boar lay in the snow.

Today the wild boar is found in southern and central Europe, south of the Baltic Sea. The head and body may measure up to 1.8 metres, and the tail may add another 25–47 centimetres. At shoulder height it will stand 90–100 centimetres. It has six incisors, a pair of canines and seven teeth in each half of the jaw; the canines extend, in the case of boars, into significant tusks and constitute its principal weapons. The European wild boar may weigh up to a remarkable 340 kg—that is for exceptionally large boars ranging the Carpathian Mountains of Poland, the former Czechoslovakia and Rumania. Such a large weight, however, falls far short of that of Big Boy—a hog bred by B. Liles and H.A. Sanders of Black Mountain, North Carolina, USA. The aptly named Big Boy tipped the scales at 1904 pounds (863 kg) on 5 January 1939.

Regarding size, the general trend appears to be that as the European wild boar spreads eastwards from its westernmost ranges it grows bigger; the same thing applies to red deer. The answer, one would think, must lie in the soil.

Bearing this in mind, then, the average weight for an adult male in Germany is about 90 kg, while in Turkey it is closer to 180 kg, and in many parts of Russia they have been reported up to 270 kg. In North America adult boars (feral) vary between 90 and 160 kg. Almost always the heavier animals bear the most resemblance to a true wild boar—that is, they are of purer breeding.

The adult wild boar is characterised by a massive body and distinctly triangular head, which extends into a significant snout. The shortish legs are slender, resulting in a minimal area of contact with the ground. Each limb terminates in four toes, of which only the two central ones actually grip the ground; the two less-developed lateral toes serve a vital purpose when the animal is in swampy terrain, where, in the manner of webbed feet, they help to prevent it sinking and drowning. The wild boar, as you will read later on, is a fine swimmer.

The overall shape of a pig's body is an evolutionary adaptation to its mostly forested habitat and allows it to move with speed through the heaviest undergrowth. Because the wild boar has been hunted by man since time immemorial—it is one of the four traditional beasts of chase—its ability to often elude those that pursue it in this type of habitat has no doubt played a vital role in the survival of the species.

The wild boar has an excellent sense of smell, keen hearing, presumably an uncanny sixth sense, but rather limited eyesight.

The pelage of a wild boar consists mostly of coarse bristles, mixed with some much finer hair. The overall effect follows no set pattern and may be grey, brown, or variegated, and, in some instances, is often quite striking. In winter, and depending on precisely where they range, they may, for further insulation, grow a thick woolly underfur. No doubt the Spanish wild pigs that range to 2700 metres in the Sierra Nevada are all in favour of such sensible insulation at such lofty heights.

The very young—called squeakers—are characterised by a short snout and alternating light and tan to dark brown bands along the length of the back; the hair has yet to coarsen and is of a silky texture. At six months of age the stripes start to fade and a year later they are attired in their final coat.

The Indian Crested Pig (*Sus scrofa cristatus*)

This particular species ranges throughout India, Burma, Malaysia and Indonesia. In India it may be found to 4500 metres in the Himalaya. A number of almost indefinable subspecies of *Sus scrofa cristatus* are found in Vietnam, Thailand, Cambodia, and many offshore islands where natives have frequently transplanted their domestic stock, which, invariably, have interbred with local wild strains.

The Indian wild pig may stand a full 101–104 centimetres at the shoulder and weigh as much as 160 kg. The species varies in colour from a reddish-brown to black, and often, in darker animals, intermingled with white. In warmer areas it may be almost devoid of hair, while in cooler climates, such as at 4500 metres up in the mountains, it is quite thickly coated.

It has been found that when an Indian wild boar mates with a domestic pig, the young of that union invariably display the characteristic longitudinal stripes of wild pigs. In 1950, T.H. Gillespie, then director of the Edinburgh Zoo in Scotland, published these relevent findings:

'We bred a number of hybrids between a male Indian wild pig and a red Tamworth sow. From the first cross we got a male that grew to a very fine beast—born in 1939, died this year.'

Apparently this boar was indistinguishable from a true wild boar of India.

Gillespie continues:

We put him to a red Tamworth sow and bred a considerable number from this cross. Of the litters, roughly about half were red and about half were darkish colour and turned the blackish grey of the typical wild pig as they matured. All were of course striped in their infancy with the white stripe of the juvenile wild pig.

For the record, the English Tamworth breed, which dates to 1812, is considered the only breed of domesticated pig which reveals its wild ancestry— that is, its snout has not shortened under domestication. The Tamworth, a common enough species in Australia's early days, is believed to revert to a feral state faster than any other breed.

Throughout its extensive range, the Indian wild boar is as destructive of crops and pastures as any animal. It is, for instance, particularly severe on sugar cane, corn, malze, millet, rice (paddy), yams/sweet potatoes, oil palm, tapioca, pineapples, coconuts and bananas. Rudyard Kipling summed it up adroitly when he said: 'The Indian pig is not exactly an important feature in agricultural life.'

As with other types of pigs, they will breed at any given time of the year, and litters on average are between eight and ten. The youngsters are mature at about a year old but do not reach full growth potential until they are around five years old, which seems to be consistent with the feral pig in Australia. The life span is thought to be about that of the European wild boar, around 20–25 years. It is highly doubtful if many pigs in the wild, due to a variety of reasons, attain such an age.

Above all else the wild boar of Asia is known for its courage, agility, and fighting prowess. The previously mentioned T.H. Gillespie wrote:

I have great respect for the courage and the leaping powers of the Indian wild pig. We once had a young one escape here and it gave us much trouble to recapture it, for it charged everybody who went near it and could leap nearly six feet high over the barriers we put up to try and corner it.

In maturity, then, standing over a metre at the shoulder and tipping the scales in excess of 130 kg, there is nothing on earth that the Indian wild boar fears in its natural environment. Even the mighty elephant avoids the mature boar; the skulking leopard, a known predator of piglets, is much too cautious to tackle him.

The tiger of course has always preyed on piglets but, as the great cat's habitat has shrunk and its numbers have become low enough for it to be considered endangered, it does not play an important role in controlling pigs any more.

However, there are on record well-documented cases of a full-grown wild boar defeating a mature tiger. How can that be? An adult male tiger will after all have an average length of 2.7 metres from nose to the tip of its tail and can be expected to weigh in the vicinity of around 180 kg. Basically, a tiger knows only one way to make a kill—that is, by leaping on the back of its prey and seizing it by the neck, and then, with violent wrenching and jerking actions, breaking the poor victim's spine. A tiger will kill a 220 kg sambar stag in this fashion, or, as has often been the case, a native villager. A domestic cat, honing those ancient instincts for when it perhaps turns feral, will use the same method of attack to kill a rabbit or hare.

The problem for a tiger when trying the same method on a boar is this: not only is the short neck extremely difficult for it to grasp in its accustomed way, but the tight-knit neck muscles of the boar, in constant use for rooting, are extremely powerful; moreover, it is not a totally petrified stag the tiger had taken on but a most ferocious beast equipped with terrible weapons like miniature swords. It is by disemboweling a tiger, or tearing open a jugular vein, that a wild boar emerges triumphant from such an encounter. The tiger is not lord of the jungle then: the wild boar is.

Another predator of the pig in parts of Asia is the jackal. Like a dingo, jackals hunt in packs. Jackals kill many piglets. However, they are no match for the mature boar and have no belly at all for a good fight.

In confrontations with man a wounded boar displays no fear whatsover. Even when a spear has penetrated its sides and it is staring death in the face, its aggression is quite extraordinary. But this of course is typical of wild pigs wherever they are found: they go down fighting.

An interesting point regarding Asian boars that inhabit regions where rattan palms grow—mainly in the East Indies—is that they are among the few wild animals in the world that will attack humans without provocation. The reason they do this is thought to be that as they forage under the rattan palms—a climbing palm with long, thin, jointed, pliable stems—they pick up needle-like thorns and become increasingly short-tempered as the tiny wounds become infected.

Fundamentally, then, the European wild boar and its close Asian relative are the not too distant forebears of the untold legions of feral pigs that inhabit various parts of the world today.

There are an estimated 26 to 28 subspecies of *Sus scrofa* worldwide (Heptner, 1966), and this includes five subspecies in what was formerly the USSR alone. A list of presently recognised subspecies can be found in the appendixes.

But wherever it is found the feral pig behaves in exactly the same fashion as its truly wild counterpart—that is, with great fortitude, with admirable bravery, and, as we shall discover further, with an amazing adaptability to a wide range of habitats.

2 In the Wild

Because of their agricultural significance, domestic pigs have been studied extensively. Research on feral pigs in Australia and the United States of America has demonstrated no major differences in the behaviour or physiology of domestic and feral pigs, so the literature on domestic pigs can be used to a reasonable degree to gain an understanding of the population biology of their free living cousins.

J.R. Giles, 1981

When north Queensland cane farmer Tony Grasso visited Lakefield National Park on Cape York Peninsula recently on a fishing trip, he expected to see plenty of pigs there. Why not? As already said, the second largest national park in the state presently carries a feral pig population about 20 000 strong.

But what the Cairns-based farmer wasn't expecting to see was a large black boar out in deep water in a billabong. A simple case of swimming wouldn't have surprised Tony Grasso in the least—pigs after all love a dip in cool, clear water. No, it was the sight of the boar diving completely under the water and then resurfacing with a big tuber in its mouth that was astounding. Moreover, the boar floated without any apparent effort on the surface of the water while it ate the tuber, the fleshy underground stem of a water lily. And once it had eaten it all up, the boar repeated the process. If Tony Grasso had not witnessed this incident for himself, he declares, he wouldn't have believed it possible.

For those of you who may not believe that a pig will kill an adult sheep just as easily as it will a new-born lamb, then the previously mentioned Graham Hardwicke tells an illuminating little story. At the time of this particular incident, Graham, then employed by the Rural Lands Protection Board, was on holiday in New South Wales. Something of a busman's holiday for he was outback once again. Just looking over the country, is the way he puts it.

Looking over the country took him to Lakemere station, out of Bourke. The property was going through a bad patch. No rain had fallen since locals couldn't really recall when. At such times the stock relied on man-made watering places to survive, as did the roos and pigs and whatever else had a raging thirst to quench. All in all a pretty typical scenario not that far from the Queensland border.

In any event, Graham was driving slowly towards a windmill when he noticed a big old ewe about to water at a lowslung wooden trough. As it did so, a black boar walked out of a patch of nearby scrub to where the sheep was drinking its fill and without any hesitation hooked its tusks into the sheep's flanks and, in Graham Hardwicke's pithy words, ' . . . ripped its guts out'. It started to feed as Graham parked some distance away. Had he shot the boar? I'd asked. No, he'd been unarmed at the time.

Arguably the omnivorous pig is the most resourceful and adaptable animal in the world. Domesticated pigs that find themselves in a wild situation for whatever reason soon revert to a feral state. The eminent scientist Charles Darwin noted with some surprise that where domestic pigs had 'gone wild' in parts of South America, the West Indies, and in the Falkland Islands, they soon dispensed with any form of their previous domesticity and reverted to the black coats, heavy bristles and large tusks of the wild boar, and the piglets to the longitudinal stripes of the wild ones.

Reversion to a feral state generally takes place quickly. It is as though the pig—in breaking all contact with man—has suddenly discovered a whole new lease of life and intends to make the most of it. Fundamentally, then, domesticity in a pig exists only while man holds it captive. Domesticity in fact is merely a glossy exterior masking the pig's quintessential wildness.

In one such recorded incident in North America, a

Left: Disturbed while wallowing, this wild boar on Hammond Downs is about to break into full flight.

Below: Extemely perceptive, pigs are acutely aware of changing climatic conditions.

A waterhole in the Adelaide River country: feral pigs were most likely well established in this watershed by the early 1870s.

terror-stricken domestic boar escaped from a burning pen and took to the nearby woods. The farmer considered it would be a simple matter to round up his pig and to drive it back to a a new enclosure; however, he was unable to locate it. Meantime, the boar found life agreeable in the woods. Why not? It was the fall, the weather was agreeable, and, because he could eat almost anything edible, and a few other morsels some might consider debatable, food was never a worry. So presumably our now gone wild boar had no intentions whatsoever of returning to his previously humdrum existence.

The farmer, however, had other ideas.

It was about two months after the boar had escaped when the farmer, a skilled hunter, finally spotted it at a wallow. He called out to the animal as he had on many previous occasions. But this time the boar did not respond in the same way. He fled in the opposite direction, as fleet as a deer, a turn of speed that astounded the farmer for he had always considered the boar a sluggish creature, dull of eye, bovine.

With full marks for persistence the farmer continued to hunt the boar. He found where it was in the habit of bedding down in a soft bed of leaves under a sheltering tree; he found another wallow. And presently he cornered the boar which displayed untold aggression toward him. Because the boar was big and strong—and did not seem like the same animal at all—the farmer feared for his life and backed away from the glowering beast. But the farmer was not done yet and enlisted the help of several neighbours. Finally the boar was captured in a net but not before it had survived an early snowfall. It was at large just eight months and perhaps for the rest of its life reflected sadly on what might have been . . .

Today, there are well-established populations of feral pigs in many parts of the world. They are found in Norway, Sweden, South Africa and the Sudan, eighteen states of mainland USA, many islands in the West Indies, Peru, Chile, Brazil, Colombia, Bolivia, Argentina, the Falkland Islands, Australia, New Zealand, numerous islands in Indonesia, Malaysia, Papua New Guinea, Fiji, Hawaii, Mauritius, and countless lesser-known islands. When all these far-flung regions are added to the already extensive range of the European wild boar and the Indian crested pig then the wild pig—that is, collectively speaking—is arguably the most widely distributed game animal in the world.

A classic example of a pig's ability to adapt to a wide variety of habitats can be found in Jamaica, where today's feral stock are directly descended from animals introduced by the Spanish in the late fifteenth century, and, partly, from domestic pigs abandoned by slaves following the abolition of slavery. Here, surrounded by the Caribbean Sea, pigs occupy a habitat that ranges from brackish, humid swamps at sea level, to the arid south coast, right up to the almost perpetually wet montane forest at altitudes of up to 1800 metres.

In 1493 Christopher Columbus made his second voyage to the New World, taking with him cattle, horses, sheep, goats, and eight pigs, these last to be liberated on islands in the West Indies as a source of food for future voyagers. In due course the pigs were put ashore. They found life agreeable in the tropics and multiplied accordingly. Not only that, they soon reverted into the kind of animal Charles Darwin would comment on. Within a mere 13 years these pigs—ranging in huge mobs—were killing cattle. Naturally enough, the islanders responded by hunting and killing those pigs responsible.

In May 1539 Hernando De Soto liberated 13 pigs in Florida. It is thought that he obtained them in Cuba, and almost certainly they were descendants of those liberated by Columbus. Just three years later they numbered 700.

Seven hundred in just three years! How and why you might well ask. To find out the reasons we need to consider the pig. Firstly it will as said eat almost anything, and this is perhaps the main reason why it survives where more selective—meaning less adaptable—animals would simply die out. Given its omnivorous nature and its intelligence, rated just below that of the great apes and far above that of the cat or dog, a pig is an animal to reckon with. To maintain its food supply it has teeth like chisels, capable of inflicting a ghastly bite, jaws that resemble a powerful vice, and an exaggerated snout that is hard and is linked by a pre-nasal bone to a very muscular neck and shoulders. The result is a perfectly designed lever that allows a pig, with little apparent effort, to break up hard-packed earth and shatter by sheer dogged persistence partly rotted logs which may harbour tempting grubs.

A pig is a most thorough chewer of its food. Interestingly enough, it will also eat the dung of other animals—if the situation is critical enough to demand it. Like domestic fowl, it has been observed to eat cow manure. A pig is able to do this because of its unique digestive system, built for survival in the harshest circumstances, which allows it to find a source of food in what others have passed through their bodies and rejected. Indeed, should a pig be confined to a yard and fed nothing but a very limited amount of grain, it will eat any faeces that contain undigested grain.

As a rule a feral sow, just like her wild ancestors, is ready to breed at around eight to ten months. The gestation period is thought to be about the same time for both wild and domestic pigs, about four months. In the course of a year a sow may have two litters—depending, of course, on whether or not conditions are favourable. There is no particular breeding time for feral pigs, so a sow may give birth at any time of the year. Because of the warmer weather, however, when there is a much lower mortality rate among new-born pigs, one is much more likely to observe a sow with young in the spring and early summer.

Seven hundred pigs from a founding stock of just thirteen in three years? Nothing to it where a feral pig is concerned, right?

In any, event a further introduction of pigs was made in Florida in 1565 by Admiral Pedro Menendez, who landed as many as 400 hogs, and sheep and horses. Typically free-ranged some of these pigs and/or their descendants came into the hands of Indians (Seminole presumably) who let them run wild in the woods where they hunted them. Less than a century later the descendants of the 1565 liberation could be found far and wide in eight large towns, 72 missions and two royal haciendas.

During the early settlement of Florida settlers raised their pigs as man had invariably done in earlier times—in a semi-wild situation. These pigs were rounded up from time to time. To avoid confusion of ownership, the law required that a hole or slit, in different arrangements, was made in each pig's ear. The pattern was then registered in the town clerk's office. The law forbade the sale of any carcass from which the ears were missing.

Today feral pigs are present in 66 of Florida's 67 counties.

In Hawaii pigs, which are thought to have arrived there with the Polynesian colonists in about AD 1000, are numerous. They cause significant damage in native forest areas—mainly by rooting up seedlings. They are also held directly responsible for the near demise of the Hawaiian goose and dark-rumped petrel.

Pigs were liberated on the island of Mauritius by a Portuguese seaman, Perdo Mascarenhas, in 1512. Among the ground birds harmed by this liberation was a very large flightless bird called the dodo. By the late seventeenth century the dodo was extinct.

Shortly after the Spanish explorer Juan de Bermudez discovered the Bermuda islands in 1515, pigs were liberated there as, again, a potential food supply for shipwrecked mariners. In 1609 English Admiral Sir George Somers was wrecked there and recorded that 'our people in the Bermudas found such abundance of hogs that for nine months' space they plentifully sufficed and yet the number seemed not diminished'. It is worth pointing out, I think, that when the Spanish took control of the Bermudas the Bermuda petrel is estimated to have numbered in excess of one million. A century later, naturalists, stunned by the damage the prolific pig was causing, considered they had gradually reduced the population to around 100 000 birds.

In 1820 the cutter *Princess of Wales* went aground on Ile aux Cochons (Pig Island) in the Indian Ocean. Her captain, C.M. Goodridge, wrote about the incident and the numbers of pigs there in his *Narrative of a Voyage to the South Seas*, published in 1834. The pigs, he said, were 'very numerous and very ferocious' and they fed mainly on the roots of tussock grasses and on seabirds, particularly penguins. Naturally enough, Ile aux Cochons became a popular spot for sealers to replenish their meat supplies—salted-down pork, one should imagine, was a particular specialty. Sir James Clark Ross wrote that, despite the best efforts of the sealers, in 1840 'you could hardly land for [pigs]'.

Pigs were released on the Galapagos Islands in about 1832. They have been particularly severe on both the giant tortoise and the East Pacific green turtle populations. Typically, they uproot the nests and feed on the eggs; with uncanny instinct they also seem to know precisely when the hatchlings are making their way to the surface and move in for the kill. Pigs are reckoned to cause a 30 per cent reduction in the annual populations of both species. Birds that suffer from pig predation on the Galapagos Islands include the Galapagos dove and the dark-rumped petrel. The Galapagos pigs also make life extremely hazardous for both land and marine iguanas. On Santiago Island, which is said to carry about 20 000 feral pigs, almost every nest on Espumilla Beach is attacked, usually within a matter of days after the iguanas start laying.

The giant monitor lizard known as the komodo dragon is found on a few islands over 1500 kilometres east of Jakarta. In 1989 wildlife officers on Komodo Island, aware that the lizards were facing extinction, put out meat for them in special places. Naturally enough the pigs found out and were soon fighting the Komodo dragons over the handout. The dragons did not come out on top.

On the Tokelau Islands pigs often find that their food supply is limited, so they turn to the sea as a source of sustenance. This most resourceful of animals wades and swims out through the shallow reef water, constantly ducking its head to feed on sea slugs and shellfish.

The French explorer Louis Antoine de Bougainville introduced pigs to the Falkland Islands in 1764. A year later Commodore John Byron, leader of a British venture, also landed pigs there, at Port Egmont. Later, pigs were liberated as an emergency food source for whalers and sealers on various lesser islands in the Falklands, namely Bleaker, Beaver, New, Quaker, Speedwell and West Point Islands. Typically the pigs did well, and, as already noted by Charles Darwin, soon reverted to a feral state. Pig-hunting became very popular among the islanders, for the skins could be exported: in 1838 about 3000 skins were sent to Great Britain. By this time huge areas of tussock land had been devastated by pigs, spelling disaster for the Magellan penguins, wild fowl, waders and petrels that had used the grasslands for shelter and nesting.

Particularly strong concentrations of feral pigs are found today in Brazil, especially in parts of the Mato Grosso, on the Bolivian border, and in the Llanos Orientale region of Colombia. In parts of Argentina they have interbred with the European wild boar, intially brought there in 1906 by rancher Pedro Luro. There are European wild boar in the states of Santa Catarina and Parana in Brazil; it should almost go without saying they have hybridised with the feral pig.

Today the most numerous of the feral ungulates in North America is—not suprisingly—the pig. They are plentiful in the southeastern and southwestern states, where they are reckoned in their hundreds of thousands. Significantly, in some states, pigs have gained game animal status. In Florida and California the annual harvest is around 100 000 animals. Without such control measures, and even allowing for a 90 per cent mortality rate among young animals, it is thought the overall population could increase by as much as 33 per cent annually. Pigs compete with native American wildlife for a valuable food source: nuts. This is a particular problem in the vast hardwood forests of California, where the species to suffer include black bear, raccoon, wild turkey, squirrel, and, hardest hit of all, white-tailed deer.

Feral pigs in North America don't have it all their own way, of course. Young (piglets) and even small pigs are preyed on by black bears, pumas, bobcats and foxes.

It has been observed that when pigs are running in the open from a predator—a puma or wolf, say—the stronger of the herd, the boars, position themselves at the fore; or if bailed up, they form a circle with the young ones in the centre. With the boars facing outwards, the would-be attacker is staring at a line of sharply honed weapons—tusks—that most likely makes it think twice before going the whole hog.

This aspect of a pig's behaviour has been taken advantage of in parts of North America where turkeys are being troubled by coyotes. Near Miles City, Montana, for instance, turkey raisers have found it profitable to have some sows and litters in the grain field they were harvesting with turkeys. When coyotes approach the sows make a great display of aggressiveness and the turkeys soon learn they are safe behind the sows, or sometimes inside a ring formed by the sows, which know full well that their young are fair game for the likes of the coyote.

Of all the animals that have been introduced into New Zealand and have reverted to a completely wild state, only the pig has become a true game animal. Although it is generally held that Captain Cook was the first European to introduce pigs into New Zealand, a French explorer, Jean de Surville, had presented two pigs to Maoris at Doubtless Bay in 1769, a good four years before Cook made his first liberation. However, as there is no record of what happened to these pigs and it is more than likely they did not survive, Cook can be said to have been responsible for the first successful introduction of pigs into New Zealand.

On 13 July 1772, on what was his second voyage to New Zealand, Captain Cook set sail from Plymouth in the *Resolution*. His consort ship, the *Adventure*, was captained by Tobias Furneaux. Among the livestock carried on both ships were pigs. On 2 June 1773 in Cannibal Cove, Queen Charlotte Sound (South Island), a boar and two breeding sows were liberated, as Cook wrote in his journal, 'so that we have reason to hope this country will in time be stocked with animals; if they are not destroyed by the natives before they become wild; for afterwards they will be in no danger. But as the natives know nothing of their being left behind, it may be some time before they are discovered.'

Cook's expedition then departed from New Zealand's shores to explore the waters to the east and north of the country. While visiting the Society Islands, he obtained as many as 300 pigs to supplement the crew's diet with fresh meat and salt pork. After stopping at Tongatapu Island in the Tongan group, Cook set sail for New Zealand once again. He had on board this time no less than 300 live fowl and about half that number of pigs.

Four of these pigs, two boars and two sows, were presented to Maoris of Cape Kidnappers, the southernmost extremity of Hawke Bay (North Island). Cook made the Maoris promise not to kill any explaining that if proper care was taken of the pigs, they would quickly multiply, and, in time, stock the whole island.

Then on 22 November 1773, back in Queen Charlotte Sound, four more pigs (one boar and three sows) were liberated. A good supply of food was left with them, enough for 10 or 12 days.

In February 1777, during his third and last voyage to New Zealand, Cook was again in Queen Charlotte Sound and gave the local inhabitants a boar and a sow. All told, Cook liberated more than a dozen pigs in New Zealand. He observed: 'It will be a little extraordinary, therefore, if this race should not increase and be preserved here, either in a wild or in a domestic state, or in both.'

The rapid dispersal of pigs in New Zealand's pre-settlement days was extraordinary. A major cause of this was the much-practised Maori custom of making large gifts—frequently a pig or pigs—to relatives and friends living with other tribes. The Maori maintained pigs in a semi-feral state, with obvious results. In inter-tribal warfare the attackers, if victorious, would seize pigs and at such times many of them would escape into the bush.

It has been said that almost every sealing and whaling ship that left New Zealand waters had on board a large number of pigs. They could fetch high prices across the Tasman, in Sydney.

By all accounts pigs were firmly established in many parts of New Zealand by 1840. Today they occur on about 28 per cent of New Zealand's total land mass.

3 Captain Cookers?

I ordered the two pigs, being a boar and sow, to be carried about a mile within the woods, at the head of the Bay. I saw them left there by the side of a fresh-water brook.

Captain James Cook, commenting on a liberation of pigs made on Bruny Island, off the coast of Tasmania, 1776

Cooktown, Cape York Peninsula, North Queensland

On a cool, overcast July morning I visited Endeavour Bicentennial Park. The gardens were well maintained, flower beds recently weeded, lawns freshly mown. There is an impressive statue of Captain James Cook erected here. The good captain looks out tirelessly over the wide Endeavour River.

On 17 June 1770 Captain James Cook, during the first of three voyages of discovery to Australian waters, found a safe haven in the bay where Cooktown now stands after his vessel, the HMS *Endeavour*, had been badly damaged on the Great Barrier Reef a week previously.

During the next seven weeks satisfactory repairs were made to the *Endeavour*. It was time not wasted inasfar as naturalist Joseph Banks and botanist Daniel Solander were concerned. They collected over 180 botanical specimens previously unknown to science. Significant too was their first encounter with the strange furry, hopping animals the natives called called *kanguru* (kangaroo).

For many years in Australia, and even today it is still a widely-held belief, it was thought that Captain Cook liberated pigs at Cooktown at the time of his 1770 visit. And that when Cook departed the pigs, typical of their race, soon became wild. Consequently, pigs became known as 'Captain Cookers'.

While Cook may have released pigs at this time, all available evidence suggests that this is not the case. The strongest argument against is, I think, to be found with the man himself, or, rather, within the pages of his meticulously kept log. Better still, a complete lack of anything to do with pigs whatsover at this particular time indicates quite clearly that they were not released here.

It is, however, an entirely different story on Cook's third voyage to Australia in 1776–80. He left England in July of that year. After calling at Cape Town, where livestock was taken onboard, including pigs, Cook was in Australian waters early in 1777.

Cook's intention was to liberate a pair of pigs on the Australian mainland for, of course, obvious reasons. But like Furneaux before him, Cook mistook D'Entrecasteaux Channel, which separates Bruny Island from the mainland, for Tasman Storm Bay, located further north. As a result, Cook liberated the pigs here, in Adventure Bay, on the eastern side of Bruny Island.

In the aftermath of seeing the boar and sow set free 'about a mile within the woods', Cook, fearful that the natives would kill the pigs, wrote, 'If ever they should meet with the pigs, I have no doubt this will be their fate. But as that race of animals soon becomes wild, and is fond of the thickest cover of the woods, there is great probability of their being preserved.'

Cook's fears for the survival of the pigs was fully justified as they are believed to have been killed by Aboriginals soon after he left there.

So while Cook's efforts to establish pigs in New Zealand almost certainly met with success, his apparently only attempt to do so in Australia failed. Be that as it may, the term 'Captain Cooker', in popular useage on both sides of the Tasman Sea, came to describe a truly wild-looking boar, invariably black, with a long pointed snout, powerful forequarters, and a sharply defined 'razorback' tapering to a comparatively slim rear-end.

4 And So, Australia

The most numerous and most disliked of Australia's feral livestock is the pig. There is probably a greater number of feral swine in the country than all other feral ungulates combined, although any estimate of the pig population is largely guesswork. In part because of this large population, but largely due to its predatory habits, the wild pig arouses more enmity and downright hatred than do the gentler species of feral livestock.

Tom McKnight, 1976

There is one thing we can be absolutely certain about: pigs arrived in Australia with the First Fleet in 1778. As with the other domesticated animals the early colonists brought with them, the pig was allowed to free range around the fast-growing settlements.

By 1795 pigs were considered such a problem at Sydney Cove that they could be legally shot if they 'trespassed on private property'. Inland, settlers also allowed their pigs to range free. In his 1827 publication *Two Years in New South Wales* P. Cunningham wrote: 'They are allowed to run in the bush during the day, just giving each a cob of maize to bring it home in the evening, if not employing a man to look after them. They feed on grasses, herbs, wild roots and native yams, on the margins of rivers or marshy ground, and also on frogs, lizards, etc., which come their way.' Then J. Henderson wrote in *Excursions and Adventures in New South Wales* (1851) that ' . . . pigs thrive and breed readily'. And, ' . . . they must, however, be allowed to run loose.'

Later, free ranging pigs became a terrible nuisance in Lonsdale Street, Melbourne, and locals considered they were as much a problem as, for instance, wild and semi-wild dingoes and dogs in other cities.

The world-wide practice of liberating pigs on uninhabited islands as a source of food for shipwrecked sailors or future settlers was soon evident in Australian waters. In 1883 the French sea captain Nicolas Baudin released pigs on Kangaroo Island off the coast of South Australia. They did so well there that within 20 years one of the island's inlets was called Hog Bay.

With the same general intentions, pigs were liberated on Flinders and French Islands in Bass Strait. Captain John Lort Stokes, commander of the HMS *Beagle* (1837–43) notes that he observed some pigs on an unnamed island in Bass Strait, and that he also saw a pair of pigs on Swan Island, located off the northeastern tip of Tasmania. Stokes saw fit to 'land a sow' on the latter named island, thus increasing the population there by, presumably, 50 per cent.

Between the years 1842 and 1846 Joseph Beete Jukes was a naturalist on HMS *Fly*, engaged on survey work in Australian waters. While off the north Queensland coast, Jukes liberated a 'pair of pigs' on an 'unrecorded' island. A year later, he returned to the same island. The two pigs had increased their numbers. Jukes records that he shot all of the pigs. No reason is given for this. Possibly Jukes, a naturalist after all, wasn't too impressed with what the pigs were doing to the environment!

In 1824 Fort Dundas was established on Melville Island, off the coast of the Northern Territory. Among other livestock, pigs were brought here. By 1826 the pigs numbered 54. The settlement on Melville Island was both short-lived and ill-fated, as indicated in this short extract from Ernestine Hill's *The Territory*.

A cyclone sweeps away the wharf, drowns the gardens, flattens the huts. The sixteen horned cattle and twenty-three sheep from Port Jackson are dead from spears and rank weed, while the four dozen pigs run wild over the island—these snouted beasts of cloven hoof the natives of the north will never eat.

In 1827 Fort Dundas was abandoned; the pigs left to their own devices and apparently eliminated by the dark-skinned locals before they really had a chance to establish themselves there.

Fort Wellington, at Raffles Bay on the Cobourg Peninsula was chosen to replace Fort Dundas. And to Fort Wellington came 20-odd pigs from Koepang, Timor. In 1929 Fort Wellington went the way of Fort Dundas. The pigs were left to fend for themselves and unharassed they multiplied and started a slow drift to the south—that is, into Arnhem Land.

Sixty-plus pigs from Kissa Island, northeast of Timor, were to be found at the Victoria Settlement at Port Essington after it was established by Captain James Bremer in 1838. Bremer also took a delivery of pigs from the south.

In 1866 the schooner *Beatrice* carried a consignment of pigs from Timor to a party of surveyors camped at Escape Cliffs, at the mouth of the Adelaide River. One of these men, a Mr Cleland, would later write ' . . . a considerable number of pigs and boars were at the same time let go. The bulk of these were crossed over the Adelaide River at the Narrows'.

Pigs were usually referred to as 'Chinese pigs' in the Top End at the time a young Norwegian student of natural history, Knut Dahl, visited there in 1894–96. In 1926 Dahl published *In Savage Australia*, in which he mentioned pigs in the Northern Territory:

> Chinese pigs ran wild, had spread over the vicinity of the Adelaide River, and multiplied exceedingly. The forests are now full of them. Everywhere along the creeks and rivers their tracks were visible, and the soil was largely turned over by their rooting.

The term 'Chinese pigs' came into common use because of the large numbers of animals imported by Chinese coolies into the Northern Territory during the gold rush of the 1850s. However it is more than likely that the pigs Dahl observed in the vicinity of the Adelaide River were descendants of Timorese, rather than Chinese, stock.

In the same publication, Dahl writes about pigs in the far north of Western Australia. For a time, again in the mid-1890s, Dahl worked on Hill station, near Roebuck Bay, north of Broome.

> My work consisted mainly of seeing that the blacks kept the troughs of the nearest wells supplied with water and that the black women watered the small vegetable garden. These duties could easily be included in my daily shooting walks.
>
> There were plenty of pigs on the station. They had been introduced some years ago, and these black Chinese pigs had, as usual, multiplied to an enormous extent. They ran wild about the place, feeding on whatever they could find, and in a wide vicinity one met them almost everywhere. In the neighbourhood of the station there were several sows with an enormous number of piglets, which constantly swarmed about the houses, eating whatever they could get. These pigs were a great asset. Almost every second morning I took my rifle and, stirring up the pigs, I quickly despatched one of the piglets. The Chinaman roasted it for dinner, and afterwards we feasted on cold pork as long as it lasted.

Around the mid-1860s many vast holdings in eastern Australia were being subdivided, and with subdivision came extensive fencing. It is thought that a great number of pigs were abandoned by their owners during this period. In other parts of the country pigs, living in a semi-feral state, simply wandered off into the bush one day and did not return. Other pigs escaped from captivity and again went wild. Man still liberated pigs wherever he went as a source of food or for sporting reasons. So by 1870—at the very latest—there were feral pig populations in many parts of the country.

After the turn of the century wild pigs increased dramatically. Well-established colonies ranged the Gascoyne, Fitzroy and De Grey rivers in Western Australia by 1911. When the government set up experimental farms in the Top End at Oenpelli (Arnhem Land), Batchelor and Daly River, this too assisted in spreading the pig. In 1918 there were sufficient wild pigs on the Finniss River for W. Powell to take up a block there and ' . . . catch pigs and carry on with mixed farming'. Out at Oenpelli, beyond the East Alligator river, buffalo shooter-cum-farmer, Paddy Cahill, reported that ' . . . the pigs are getting wild as the natives do a lot of killing among them'.

Apparently, free-ranging pigs, following the watercourses, first arrived in Queensland's Channel Country—the Diamantina and Georgina rivers—between 1913 and 1921. With time, the Queen state became the main haven of wild pigs in Australia and eventually they were found in varying densities over almost all of the state.

Most certainly pigs increased their numbers and extended their range during the Second World War, a period when suitable manpower to control them was in extremely short supply. The situation was summed up in an article titled 'Wild Pigs', published in *Walkabout* magazine in 1943:

> They have wiped out several species of ground birds in North Queensland, and have taken a heavy toll of the

marsupials. But it is on the cattle stations and farms that they have done the most damage, by rooting up crops, ruining pastures, killing calves and valuable dogs, and destroying fences.

The trend for pigs to establish new colonies continued. By the early-to-middle 1950s they were more widespread in Western Australia and Victoria, and were penetrating into the more mountainous regions—that is, parts of the Great Dividing Range where they had never been seen before. Due to a number of mild seasons they spread into the Hillston and Cobar districts of New South Wales, and extended their range north of the Darling River system to the Queensland border. And even in Queensland new populations were springing up where previously pigs were unheard of. At Cunnamulla is one example. Again, they were on the move in the Northern Territory.

Certainly by the end of the 1950s the feral pig was recognised as being this country's most pernicious pest—found guilty of not one but many unforgiveable crimes.

Make no mistake about it, the feral pig found in Australia is a predator. By any reckoning a supreme predator. It will prey on lambs, adult sheep, foals, calves, kids and poultry. It will, should the opportunity arise, kill bigger animals than these—sick or injured animals or perhaps those bogged and unable to defend themselves properly. It also preys on small native fauna: both mammals and ground-nesting birds.

Also high on the list of pigs' transgressions is damage to fencing, either that used to contain stock or animals regarded as pests—the dingo, for instance. In areas of low rainfall, where water is vital for the survival of stock, they are especially severe on dams, tanks, water troughs, drains, and so on. And they wallow and root in natural waterholes and billabongs, turning them boggy, which may cause stock to become trapped there, possible targets not only for the pigs themselves but for the watchful dingoes, which often follow cattle.

The feral pig also has a significant impact on crops, including wheat (wheat growers in New South Wales experience the greatest damage), maize, sorghum (especially in parts of Queensland), cotton, rice, sugarcane (as early as the 1930s the sugarcane industry in Queensland had introduced special regulations to deal with pigs), bananas, soya beans and vegetables, with potatoes especially favoured.

Basically, pigs in this country are found to feed on all types of seed, grain, fruit and vegetable crops with the marked exception of safflower, a thistle-like plant with flowers used for dye or oil.

To combat pigs—and to provide an incentive to hunt them—the Department of Lands in Queensland was possibly the first such organisation to implement a bounty system with payment for tokens (ears). It is possible, however, and very likely as a matter of fact, that some stationmen paid out a bounty for 'rogue' pigs long before this.

Be that as it may, the bounty system seems to date to the early 1930s in Queensland. Over the next 40 years the department paid out bonuses on very nearly 2 million pigs, representing an annual figure of around 47 000. In one financial year alone—1957–58—the bonuses claimed amounted to 131 740. Undoubtedly a great many pigs were killed in the Queen State and not claimed for.

The year 1957 also happened to be a most lucrative one for hunters in the Walgett (New South Wales) district, because the local Pastures Protection Board paid out bonuses on 21 567 pigs.

An interesting list compiled by Tom McKnight in 1976 relates to problems caused by pigs and also includes some details of bonus payments in a number of districts in New South Wales in 1961 (see page 35).

Due to good breeding seasons, the pig population in the Top End's Daly River country 'exploded' in the early-to-mid 1960s. The same thing may well have happened in the Kimberleys of Western Australia.

At any rate, three government shooters went to just one station on the banks of the Daly in 1966 and over three days shot 2500 pigs, with a best day's tally of 600. Three years later a further control programme took place on the same property eliminated an 'estimated' 90 per cent of the pig population.

Then in late 1972, during a similar programme, 1200 pigs were taken. Two sites were used for this particular shoot: where the 1966 and 1969 control measures had taken place, and at a place where no regulated hunting had been carried out. The men involved with this shoot considered there were 'about' equal numbers of pigs at both sites. This clearly indicates that a 90 per cent reduction in pig numbers is effective for less than three years. This is the fundamental problem of controlling pig populations: in good conditions their populations can escalate by as much as 500 per cent in a 12–15 months period.

For the record, the local Primary Industry

In the watershed of the East Alligator River in Arnhem Land the feral pig found perfect habitat.

Top: Aborigine hunting spear (from Arnhem Land).

Bottom: The East Alligator River

Foraging at a billabong in the East Alligator River Watershed.

Typical red soil country in far western New South Wales (northeast of Broken Hill).

Left: Patrolmen Peter (foreground) and Charlie Russell repairing the Dingo Fence (called the Border Fence locally) in southwest Queensland. Feral pigs are one of a number of animals that cause extensive damage to the longest man-made fence in the world.

Ray Jones checking out the bed/nest of a feral pig in the Macquarie Marshes most likely used by a sow with young.

Below: Feral pigs in the marshlands.

Above: Spoor of wild pig.

Left: Tony Grasso indicating pig tracks on his sugarcane farm at Cairns.

Below: Tony Grasso pointing to the high rainforest where the pigs that raid his sugarcane farm mostly live.

Bonus payments and reported pig problems, 1961

Pastures protection district	Reported pig problems	Situation regarding bonus payments
Bourke	Lamb losses, Damage to bore drains	P.P Board pays 2/6 per scalp; 6800 per year bountied the last 2 years
Brewarrina	Lamb losses, Fouling water supplies	
Broken Hill	No pigs in district	
Canonba	Damage to fences, Many other problems	
Cobar	Some lamb losses, Some loss of weak ewes, Not serious at present	
Condobolin	Little problem, as few pigs are present	
Coonamble	Heavy lamb losses, Damage to fences, Damage to bore drains	
Deniliquin	Few pigs in district; no damage reported	Some stations pay bonuses
Hay	Damage to fencing, Lamb losses	
Milparinka	Few pigs in district; no damage reported	
Moree	Lamb losses Damage to crops	Some stations pay bonuses
Narrabri	Few pigs in district; no extensive damage	
Pilliga	10% lamb loss, Crop damage, 5–10% of yield	P.P. Board pays 1/6 per scalp
Walgett	Lamb losses, Damage to tanks and bore drains, Rooting out of natural grasses	P.P. Board pays 1/- per scalp; 5700 per year bountied for last 4 years
Walgett North	Lamb loss, 30–40%, Damage to tanks and bore drains, Rooting out of grasses	P.P. paid 2/- per scalp prior to 1957; now pays 2/6 per scalp; 13 000 per year bountied for last 6 years
Wentworth	No reported damage	
Wilcannia	No recent damage reported	

Department in the Northern Territory estimated their pig population at somewhere between 100 000 and 200 000 animals.

The predatory nature of the pig is perhaps never better exemplified than when it kills livestock. The following chilling incident is told by an anonymous sheepman from the Ilfracombe district in Queensland:

Pigs are a very real menace in this area. Many people who do not have any experience of pigs in their wild state find it hard to believe the incredible damage they can cause among vulnerable sheep. Oddly enough, sheep seem to have no fear of pigs, which is a fact exploited to the full by any cunning old pig. I remember watching

a mob one day, per medium of field glasses at a considerable distance, in a state of helpless rage, while a medium sized boar, an old sow, and a litter of half grown suckers attacked, killed, and ate half a dozen merino lambs, ranging in size from three weeks to nearly two months old. The pigs as a mob were rooting for grass roots and insects on a flat by a creek, and sheep were moving across this flat, feeding out from water in the late afternoon. The pigs were scattered over a fair area, and the sheep would feed up to and mingle with them as they moved out. Whenever a feeding ewe and lamb came anywhere near either of the two adult pigs, there would be a quick dash and the body of the lamb would go up in the air, kicking, to fall to the ground and be torn to pieces by the pigs. There would be a momentary scatter among the sheep, and then the peaceful feeding away from water process would resume, and a few minutes later the pigs would have another lamb.

And from the same state, but this time from Cunnamulla, another grazier commented that:

The pig is not a spectacular killer like the dingo, and the damage he does is not sufficiently recognized. This is mainly due to the fact that very little is left of a lamb. Usually only a few chips of bone and a little wool. Only those people who have seen pigs kill and then viewed the practically nonexistent remains realize the extent of undetected losses due to this predator.

And how, you might wonder, do pigs deal with cattle? Well, in his book *The Spurs Are Rusty Now* R.H. Conquest, while working on a big station in Queensland's Georgina River Country (near the Northern Territory border) wrote in his typically succinct but graphic fashion: 'The wild pigs, especially the big boars, were terrors on young calves. They'd run them down, just for the hell of it, and slash them to pieces with their tusks.'

Living in the wild, a pig has three main requirements: a dependable supply of water, protection from extremes of temperature, and seclusion. And for preference a clean dry bed in every season.

The preferred habitat of feral pigs is never far from water, and, as a rule, they are not found more than 2 kilometres from it. Indeed, they were once nicknamed 'watercourse' in parts of Queensland.

The expression 'to sweat like a pig' is at best an inappropriate one. It has been recently discovered that pigs can't sweat, or at least not significantly. By comparison, human beings cool themselves by sweating, evaporating as much as 1000 grams of body liquid per hour for each square metre of body surface; while a pig can only manage 30 grams per square metre. So a pig in the harsh Australian hinterland where summer temperatures climb extremely high has no choice but to live near water. It must in such conditions drink frequently, and it must wallow in water or mud.

During a 4-year programme on feral pigs carried out by the NSW Department of Agriculture, it was found that:

The importance of water cannot be overstressed. In western New South Wales in summer the pig that cannot wallow at least once a day is in trouble. Dehydration and hyperthermia kill and kill quickly. As an example most pigs that were held in the open at temperatures of 35°C without wallowing water died within 12 hours.

However, drought is not thought to have any real impact on pig numbers as they are able to locate sufficient water in man-made dams, tanks and troughs. The hard times mean there is more carrion around than normal for them to feed on.

But of course with drought conditions come bushfires. In Victoria, for instance, a large number of pigs living in the Otway Forest on the headwaters of the Gellibrand River were completely wiped out when a major bushfire swept through in 1938–39.

And yet even such natural control methods as flooding work to the long-term benefit of the feral pig. In the aftermath of flooding, which often follows a period of drought, comes renewed growth, often quite luxuriant. In such ideal breeding conditions pigs multiply rapidly.

In 1971 there was severe flooding in the Barwon/Namoi/Castlereagh river systems in northern New South Wales and the general opinion was that feral pigs had all but been eliminated. Within a period of only two years there were so many pigs there—even more than before—that bewildered farmers in the district had to organise shooting parties. Despite the fact that many pigs are drowned when severe flooding occurs, they are excellent swimmers and take to the water readily both for pleasure and, if the situation demands it, to escape from danger.

Charles Lyell, a naturalist, reported that in the great floods which took place in Scotland in 1829 many domestic animals were drowned. As for pigs, well 'one pig only six months old swam four miles and landed safe', and 'three others of the same age and litter swam at the same time five miles to the west and landed at Backhill'. Lyell believed that in an adult and wild state the animals would have been stronger and more active 'and might, when pressed, have performed a much longer voyage'.

Lyell's travels took him far afield from his native Scotland, and in 1869, on the subject of wild pigs in the Java/Moloccus region, he wrote, 'They swam with ease and swiftly for many miles at sea.' When Lyell was later questioned on this point, he replied that the observations were his own and did the doubting Thomas wish to question them further?

In the mid-1870s two British zoologists, Thomas Pennant and Alfred Russel Wallace, credited the wild pig with extraordinary swimming prowess. Pennant, for instance, stated that New Guinea supplied all of the South Sea Islands with pigs that 'swam from island to island', and Wallace, finding pigs all over the Malay Archipelago, attributed their wide dispersal to the same ability.

Favourable conditions naturally aid with the dispersal of pigs on dry land. In 1974 heavy rains caused Lake Eyre to flood for the first time since European occupation of this country. The receding floodwaters lured pigs down to this lake from their previous known range limit—the Channel Country— and that is how they came to inhabit territory where they were once unknown.

Still with 1974 very much in mind, in Canberra, I talked at some length with Dr John McIlroy of the CSIRO. In the course of our conversation he mentioned a very interesting story which, in later correspondence, he clarifed somewhat:

Enclosed are the references on feral pigs you were interested in. As far as I know Ross Bryan of the Conservation Commission of the Northern Territory has still not published his work with Judas pigs near Alice Springs, so I will provide the following summary from a letter he sent to me.

'Some time in 1974, two boars and five sows escaped from Amoonguna Aboriginal settlement 14 kms east of Alice Springs into the Todd River Floodout on Undoolya Station. During the seventies the Central Australian district experienced good falls of rain, making conditions ideal for the pigs with natural food and water plentiful throughout the area. Several control methods were carried out over the years.' These included trapping, using various types of baits and shooting, both on the ground, with dogs, and from helicopters. 1080 poisoning was not attempted because it is not an acceptable method in the NT.

All the techniques proved unsuccessful, so they caught 2 sows, by flushing them out of thick undergrowth, into a circle of blokes on the ground. They then fitted these pigs with radio transmitter collars and released them. From then on they flew over the area in a helicopter every 2 weeks or so, located the Judas pigs, shot any other pigs associated with them and left the Judas pigs to move on and regroup with the other pigs. After 11 fiights they had shot 45 pigs and since then they have found no evidence (ground and air patrols) of feral pigs still in the area.

The above account may, I think, serve very well as a telling example of how difficult it is to eradicate even a small number of pigs in a comparatively small area of country. Only by using devious methods once unheard of in animal control, and at great cost to the taxpayer, was the object finally achieved.

An estimation of the feral pig population in Australia on a state by state basis was made by Tom McKnight in 1976.

Queensland	300 000	to	1 000 000
New South Wales	100 000	to	300 000
Northern Territory	50 000	to	100 000
Western Australia	15 000	to	40 000
Victoria	5000	to	15 000
South Australia	2000	to	10 000
Tasmania	1000	to	5000
Total	473 000	to	1 470 000

In commenting on these findings, McKnight wrote:

A determination of the approximate number of feral swine in Australia requires even more guesswork than with the other species surveyed. This is primarily because of the rapid fluctuations that can occur from one season to another, particularly in response to weather. The totals shown are crude estimates and are designed to represent an average between drought and non-drought extremes. The only certainty is that feral pigs are numbered in the hundreds of thousands, even in bad years.

Later research into Australia's feral pig population clearly indicates that McKnight's findings were on the conservative side, for in 1980 Dr P.M. Flynn came up with a grand total of 8–11 million pigs nationwide. Flynn reached this staggering number by considering that 5 million pigs were in Queensland, 3–5 million in New South Wales, 200 000 in the Northern Territory, about 500 000 in Western Australia, and 2000 elsewhere, including on offshore islands.

Among those who considered McKnight's figure was a 'major underestimate' and that Flynn's conclusions 'may be on the high side' was C.A. Tisdall. Tisdall estimated that there were 3–6 million pigs in this country for the same general period.

It is well worth taking into account that within this same timespan the feral pig may well have been on the increase in various parts of the country— certainly these are the findings of J. Hone and J. Waithman in an article titled 'Feral pigs are spreading', published in the *Agricultural Gazette* (New South Wales, 1979). Perhaps R.S. Cutler took this into consideration when in 1989 he calculated there were 8–12 million feral pigs in Australia.

Approximate range of the feral pig in Australia (adapted from C. A. Tisdall's *Wild Pigs: Environmental Pest or Economic Resource?* Pergamon Press, 1982)

Realistically, it is of course impossible to state with any real degree of accuracy precisely how many wild pigs there are in Australia. Fundamentally, this is because their numbers are governed by environmental influences, and as a direct consequence are always fluctuating, often quite dramatically.

But nevertheless such surveys are vitally important and they do prove that Australia's feral pig population is a formidable one, that they range from the tropics to the snowline, and that in the 1990s they occupy about 38 per cent of the overall landmass of the largest island continent on earth.

PART TWO
IN TROPIC REGIONS

5 Cropraiders

Tony Grasso, a 54-year-old first-generation Australian, paused as we walked side by side along a muddy track at the back of his 170-acre sugar cane farm on the outskirts of Cairns and gestured emphatically towards a densely-forested range of low hills his property backed against. He then explained in a heavily resigned voice, as though he had said it a thousand times before, that was where the pigs that raided his crops usually lived.

It was rainforest country up there, a part of the Great Dividing Range. Tony said it was now a World Heritage Area.

We carried on, watching where we put our feet. It was supposed to be the dry season up here but no one had bothered to tell Mother Nature that. Still, it was a very lovely evening, with the sun sliding towards the hills.

. 'Hey, look here,' said Tony a few minutes later. He dropped to one knee and, using a forefinger, pointed at the unmistakeable spoor of a pig. He looked up at me; his eyes were very brown. 'When d'you think this was made?' The tone of his voice made the question seem like some sort of test.

I considered the hoofmark: cleanly etched in the rich dark soil. I said, 'Overnight . . . maybe this morning.' I made eye contact with him.

Tony smiled and bobbed his head. 'Right, last night.'

'Fair-sized pig.'

He nodded again. 'Yeah—a sow.' He straightened. About middle height, stocky build, thick grey hair. He looked fit. A wry expression crossed his darkly tanned Mediterranean features. 'We've been here for twenty years now and there's always'—an expressive lift of his solid shoulders—'been troubles with pigs.' By 'we' Tony meant his wife, Rose. 'Dad had his problems with pigs as well,' he continued, 'but not to the extent we've had here.' Tony's father had come out from Italy to the land of opportunity after the First World War, and had taken up a sugar came farm at Hawking's Creek, near Ingham.

Again Tony indicated the rain forest. 'The pigs tend to stay there during the wet but when that's over they start coming down here. It's very difficult to hunt them in the forest—it's so thick.' He pulled a face. 'Dogs don't do much better in the cane, either.' I could see what he meant: the cane stood about 2 metres high and was densely interlocked, the leaves tangled, sharp of edge. Taipan territory.

I paused. More tracks in the muddy ground. A set of medium-sized prints, some smaller ones. Tony considered them, too.

'There's gotta be a boar and a couple of sows and their young ones here permanently—that is, it's their home territory.'

I caught his eye. 'You mentioned dogs. What other methods have you tried to get rid of them?'

He shrugged. 'The usual. Shooting, traps, poisons.

The trouble is that once you put the pressure on them—and perhaps get a dozen or so—the rest shift camp and you won't see them for quite some time.'

Again we stopped: I saw where pigs crossed a small watercourse on a regular basis, the coarse grass bent over, particles of dried mud clinging tenaciously to it. At this point the pigs had crossed the track and made inroads into the cane via a low tunnel.

'They can be in there,' said Tony, meaning the cane, 'and you'll never know it. They'll eat out a few acres in a matter of days, no worries. Pigs in the cane make mechanical harvesting difficult. They roll about in it too and make nests.'

I nodded. Once pigs develop a liking for cane they seem to find it pretty much irresistible and they will raid crops on a regular basis. Basically, they tend to chew the cane well, extracting the juice, and then spitting out much of the fibre. An illuminating aspect of pigs in Queensland is that high populations inhabit coastal regions where sugar cane is a prime industry.

We continued and at a recently used pig wallow, located just off the track Tony explained that as an incentive to control pigs the Cane Pest and Disease Control Boards paid a bounty of $10 per head. The token was a set of ears and, as a rule, Tony waited until he'd got perhaps seven or eight dried tokens before he cashed in. The scheme had been running for many years in Queensland and it was operated locally by an officer based at the Mulgrave mill (Tony's farm was within the Mulgrave Shire).

With evening starting to draw in, we turned away from the wallow which later on, perhaps, would be put to good use. I noticed a stand of fruit trees nearby. Mangoes, Tony said. Pigs? Tony smiled ruefully. Once the fruit started to drop on the ground you had to beat off the pigs with a stick, they loved it that much. At other times, he went on, he'd grown watermelons and pumpkins but, as he'd soon discovered that was a bad mistake for there really wasn't anything you could grow in north Queensland that a pig wouldn't eat. Tony Grasso of Italian extraction was not wrong there.

Fringing Mission Beach, south of Cairns, is a 40-acre block upon which bananas have been grown for over 30 years. The land was all scrub when Laurie Porter took it on in the early 1960s—the job of clearing it for cultivation was, he now says, backbreaking. But clear it they did. Today Laurie, while still very active, is semi-retired and the farm is looked after by his sons, Danny and Max.

One Sunday evening, I was sitting with Laurie on the weather-worn veranda of the old homestead. We were enjoying a beer. Across the main road into Mission Beach—no real distance away—was some of the banana crop. A vehicle roared past—a busy road, Laurie said.

The banana crop was laid out in orderly rows, the trees taller than I had expected, the lowering sun fired them so that they profiled with a three-dimensional effect.

Beyond the banana trees stood the rainforest. Beyond the rainforest lay a wide belt of marshlands. And beyond the swamps was the coastline. It was, Laurie said, about a mile to the coast from here. He did not tell me, and I did not need to be told, that it was great country for pigs in there.

Laurie sipped his beer. The brutal sun had left its mark on his skin. A reflective expression crossed his craggy features as he considered my question. He put down his can of beer on a table. He smiled wryly.

'Pigs, you say? Yeah, we've had our problems with them, all right. They're really a way of life around here, you could say. Just about everyone I know who's growing bananas has their problems with pigs.

I listened quietly while Laurie expanded on the subject of wild pigs in the district, wondering as he spoke in such a matter-of-fact way how anyone could put up with the same set of problems each year, three decades in all.

He told me that pigs came through the block most nights and that they ate whatever bunches of bananas had fallen to the ground—green or ripe, no matter. The bigger pigs were able to reach up—by jumping up and placing their front feet firmly on the trunk—and yank down a bunch. A large boar, for instance, could reach to about two metres above ground level. Higher than that? They had an answer to that, no worries. They used either tusk or teeth, or a combination of both in the case of a boar, to simply destroy the tree just above ground level. Down with a crash came the tree. Whole bunches of tempting bananas just waiting to be eaten. During one period some years ago when they were particularly troublesome, Laurie had seen as many as 20 mature trees destroyed in this fashion. Moreover, they dug up the ground, frequently undermining both mature and young trees, so that they too came down in a heap. There was no real end to it, Laurie finished.

'Another?' He indicated my empty can.

'Like to but you know how it is . . . ?'

'Sensible.' He smiled. 'But as I'm not driving anywhere . . . ' He busted open another can of Queensland's finest.

After a lengthy interval, Laurie said:

'Course the boys've got electric fencing around them now but there's a big fella that jumps'—he swung a big, work-hardened hand in the direction he meant—'the fence over there.' He shook his head. 'Proving rather hard to get that one.' The boar had apparently been visiting the farm overnight for about a month, they thought, and they knew him only by the size of his hoofmark and a few strands of coarse black hair caught up in the fencing—a calling card, if you like.

Laurie stood up suddenly, tall and almost gaunt:

'That boar's gotta go 350 pounds at least,' was his summing up of the unseen animal's size. 'See that pineapple crop over there? Well, some years ago a fair-sized boar was getting in there every night and doing heaps of damage: they like pineapples when they're about two-thirds grown for some reason. Dunno why, they just do.

'Anyway, I put an electric fence around the entire crop, thinking that'd stop him. Stop him? Like hell it did! The bugger must've stood back and then charged the fence and taken the whole lot with him, y'know, 'cause in the morning it was all tangled up in the middle of the patch and God only knows how many pineapples he and his mates ruined that night.'

Pineapples?

One year Laurie had put in 5000 pineapple plants. He had watched them grow to near maturity—that is, about two-thirds of their potential. Then to his great dismay he had seen every single pineapple systematically destroyed. He'd pretty much given up on growing pineapples large scale after that disaster.

Out at Wandinya farm on the western side of the Northern Territory's Adelaide River, Ken Sheriden,

50, knows all about the frustrations of growing bananas in wild pig country, too.

The lean, leathery West Australian came to the 10 000 acre property in 1985, where they also grow rice, mangoes, plant hay.

'At least they don't bother the cattle,' said Ken drily.

'Ten thousand acres,' I mused aloud. 'Surely you'd call that a station rather than a . . . '

'Always been called a farm,' Ken said with a decisive shake of his head, 'even when it was much bigger.'

Well, fair enough.

Soon about eight pigs—a sow and suckers, Ken reckoned—were making regular overnight forays into the banana crops, despite the fact it was fenced off with barbed wire.

'Once they get a taste for them . . . ' Ken raised eyebrows spoke volumes for the sheer persistency of a determined pig. 'It's the same thing with mangoes too, just like that fella in Queensland you were telling me about. We tried rock melons once . . . ' He shook his head as though that was a particularly bad memory.

'You mentioned rice?'

He smiled without a trace of humour. 'Rice? Yeah, well that's another bad one, no mistake. They go through a crop like a plough—you'd have to see it to believe it, mate. The worst thing is that they'll flatten an entire crop just to get at the heads of the grain. Rice? They just love the stuff.'

While Ken was telling me all this, a brownish dog of medium size was close at hand. Her name, Ken said at my interest, was Toffy. And she, just like pigs, craved bananas. In a single day—each and every day—she would eat between 20 and 30 large bananas. But she wasn't fat? No, that was because of her predominantly Dingo blood, for, like a terrier, she was almost always on the move.

6 The Pig and the Cassowary

Six landowners blamed the decline of the cassowary directly on the pig. A regional Inspector employed by the LPB has observed cassowary chicks being consumed by feral pigs. Although the actual cause of death could not be attributed to pig predation, the freshness of the carcass and fresh blood in the vicinity would lead to the assumption that predation by pigs was the cause of death.

Jim Mitchell, Department of Lands,
Charters Towers, 1976

Upwind, the smallish black pig was momentarily unaware of the vehicle fast approaching it. In rainy conditions, the feral one's attention was intent upon rooting up the rich black soil fringing the unsealed coastal route in Queensland's Cape Tribulation National Park. Suddenly the pig jerked up its head and then bolted into the forest.

Not much further on from where the pig had left its tell-tale evidence of upturned earth was a roadsign not seen anywhere in this country but in the tropical rainforests of northeastern Queensland. It warned motorists of the presence of a large, flightless bird: the cassowary.

So pigs and cassowaries share a common ground. On one hand we find a feral animal detested by conservation groups and on the other an almost revered species of native bird. A logical question that springs readily to mind is precisely how does the feral pig affect the cassowary. Does the pig, for instance, feed heavily on the eggs of the bird? Does the pig prey heavily on chicks? Can the pig be blamed directly for the apparent decline in the numbers of cassowaries? To find out the answers to these and other relevant questions, I considered it pertinent to make contact with Joan Bentrupper Baumer, a biologist working mainly in rainforest ecology and animal behaviour.

Based at lovely Mission Beach, Joan first began work on the cassowary in 1986. This was a direct result of a major cyclone which came through much of the cassowaries' range—that is, from about north of Townsville to the tip of Cape York Peninsula— and within this comparatively narrow coastal belt where the species is found an incredible amount of the forest was totally defoliated. The consequences of Cyclone Winifred, to give the destructive female her name, was that people living in and around Mission Beach, prime cassowary habitat, soon noticed that a large number of the birds were coming out of the devastated rainforest and into urban areas to be hand-fed. Obviously the species faced a serious problem.

At any rate, this is where the Queensland National Parks and Wildlife Service, along with CSIRO, comes into the picture. They instigated a research programme on cassowary biology and distribution, and who better to call on for assistance than Joan Bentrupper Baumer.

Presently Joan, working fulltime on the cassowary project, found herself with a research area that covered 200 square kilometres, within which were study sites. The job demanded long hours in the field, often in rainy conditions. But she found it both rewarding and stimulating.

It soon became apparent to her that feral pigs were plentiful all over her area of research; indeed, she was to see many while searching for and observing cassowaries.

So is the pig a major threat to the very survival of the cassowary as some people think it is? I would put to her at her beachfront home.

To date, Joan has seen no evidence whatsoever to support a claim that pigs feed on the eggs of the cassowary, as, for instance, they do in the case of the brush-turkey. The reason for this is that the brush-turkey, in the manner of a saltwater crocodile, makes a mound-like nest and relies on whatever vegetable matter is piled upon the eggs to generate enough heat

Banana crop on Laurie Porter's block. Ripe or green, pigs love bananas.

Ken Sheridan and someone else who loves bananas—Toffy, the dingo cross.

Above: Roadsign warning motorists of the presence of cassowaries—Cape Tribulation National Park, Cape York Peninsula.

Left: Cassowary, north of Cairns.

Below: Trapped!

as it decomposes to incubate them eventually.

On the other hand, the cassowary makes a simple nest: a mere scrape in the ground. The nest site is normally deep in the rainforest. The nest itself is lined with grasses, fern fronds and leaves. The female lays the eggs, normally four, and it is then the responsibility of the male bird to incubate them. So diligent is he in regard to this responsibility that, according to Joan, he does not leave the nest site. Incubation takes around 56–60 days.

By all accounts, the male cassowary does not like intruders at the place he sits. He is also an aggressive bird with, in some instances, a hair-trigger temper. To go with a belligerent nature is sheer size: they may stand 1.5–2.0 metres in height, and, physically, are more thickset than an emu. Also they are well-armed by way of a large, straight claw, rather like a marlinspike, attached to the inside toe of each foot. The foot is linked with an extremely powerful leg. Consequently, they fight with their feet. They could quite literally kick or pound a potentially egg-stealing snake or goanna to death, and they would certainly raise enough ruckus to make even a big pig rethink the situation. Personally, I think a pig would have too much sense to bother itself with a nesting cassowary that would certainly turn aggressive if warranted. The coastal belt they both occupy, and have been doing successfully for a very long time (135 years?), is very much like a larder that is always full where the omnivorous pig is concerned. But an abandoned nest site, with eggs invitingly exposed, would of course be an entirely different story.

Once the male cassowary has successfully incubated the eggs the chicks—in the manner of all ground-nesting birds—are mobile. The female bird is still absent from the scene and the male bird now has the job of raising the young ones. People who have approached a male bird in this situation know how very dangerous they can be. In New Guinea, for instance, where hunting the cassowary is a way of life, native tribesmen have been killed by the male bird protecting its young. There is one such recorded fatality in this country.

All going well the male cassowary looks after the chicks until they are about nine months old and then leaves them to fend for themselves. But should a serious injury or even death befall the male cassowary while the young are still defenceless, then once again they are indeed vulnerable to not only the pig but other predators too.

Basically, then, it cannot be stated that the pig is a direct threat to the survival of the cassowary: if that were the case the bird would have been on the endangered list years ago. Rather, the pig is an indirect threat to its eventual survival, and that is entirely due to the manner in which man retaliates when pigs undermine his very livelihood.

As already said, pigs and cassowaries inhabit lowland coastal regions of north Queensland. Running parallel to the pig/cassowary range are a great many agriculture areas, mostly sugar cane and bananas. Farmers try and control pigs here by three methods: trapping, shooting and dogging. The problem is that in trying to eradicate an introduced species they were causing a lot of problems for a native species, namely the cassowary.

Let's look at traps for openers.

A Pestfact Information Bulletin—'Control Of Feral Pigs'—has this to say about traps/trapping:

> Trapping can be an important technique for reducing feral pig numbers and is most successful when the pigs' food resources are limited. Pig traps are species specific and pose little or no danger to other wild or domestic animals.
>
> There are several trap designs but all are principally a steel mesh, live trap with a one-way gate. Free feeding prior to activating traps is an essential prerequisite to successful trapping.
>
> Bait for traps, which are attractive to feral pigs, include wheat, sorghum, corn, potatoes, apples, oats, barley and bread. Sheep, kangaroo, cattle or pig carrion is a good lure, and areas containing old carcasses on which pigs have been feeding for some time are useful places to set traps.

Obviously not included in the above list of foods that act as a tempting lure for pigs were bananas, which, in this particular instance, were what local farmers baited their pig traps with.

And therein lay a problem.

In its natural situation a cassowary feeds heavily on fruit that may fall from certain rainforest trees and vines. Also, the cassowary—just like the pig—is a cropraider. So when the food supply runs short in the forest, or perhaps when they simply fancy a change of diet, they will make forays into gardens and orchards eating such fruit as mulberries and, in particular, bananas. Obviously, then, a pig trap baited with rotting bananas would not only attract pigs but cassowaries too. And this is precisely what was happening at the time Joan began her research on the cassowary.

Laurie Porter (previous chapter) told me that in trying to control pigs on his block he had often baited traps with bananas, the best bait of all, he reckoned. But had he sometimes trapped a cassowary in such a trap? Yes, he admitted, he had. And? Well, they had released the bird next morning, unharmed. But as Joan Bentrupper Baumer knows only too well—it is not as simple as that.

For not all traps are checked each morning. They should be but they are not. It might, in some cases, be a matter of days before someone does the right thing. In this instance a trapped cassowary will die— of shock, most likely. Joan believes that this type of thing has happened far too often in north Queensland.

The local farmers main response to dealing with pigs was of course a nationwide one: they called on the services of men using trained dogs. This is how Laurie Porter and Tony Grasso, the sugar cane farmer near Cairns, have faced the pig problem, Laurie over 30-odd years, and Tony for 20 years.

'Yes, dogs are a major threat where cassowaries are concerned,' Joan says. 'Particularly packs of dogs. Some pighunters are excellent in terms of control over their dogs but others . . . ' She shrugged a slim shoulder expressively and didn't have to add anything to that. She also mentioned that hunters without dogs caused problems, too, inasmuch as some of them were not selective in what they shot. That was also true.

We had been talking, I realised, for well over an hour.

'What about the future?' I asked.

'How do you mean?'

'The pig/cassowary relationship, if you like.

She pondered that for a moment. Then: 'There's little point, I think, in putting massive amounts of money and resources into a programme whereby one believes the pig can be eradicated: it's almost impossible to do that and a number of research programmes have been done on it and have come up with those conclusions.

'The real problem when you're looking at conserving a native endangered species—and particularly when you are dealing with a community—is that you have to put in place a system whereby they identify the real threatening process to the survival of that species.

'Certainly there are a number of minor effects—I call them that but to some people they may be major—such as dogs, pigs, roads and hand-feeding— that have an impact on cassowary survival. What you

have to be most careful about is that you do not direct the public into putting all their emphasis on just one of those aspects rather than the real issue which is loss of habitat.

'So at the moment my main concern is that with the 'pig issue' being so topical all the money and resources that are presently available are going to be put into dealing with pigs, because that is not the major problem where the cassowary is concerned.'

In any event, I drove away from Joan Bentrupper Baumer's place, heading for a golden stretch of sand —the beach at Mission Beach.

What a realist she was, I thought, in the way she had summed up the feral pig situation—yes, much more sensible to learn to live with them than entertaining totally unrealistic thoughts about trying to eliminate such an enterprising species.

It was good, too, that Joan did not look upon feral pigs with loathing as many diehard conservatives are apt to do. Rather she seemed to accept them for what they were and, I suspect, she had a soft spot for the animals that share the habitat of the cassowary. Certainly she had not been threatened by pigs in the many encounters she had had with them. Perhaps it was the way in which she'd related the following incident—with humour and no little wonder—that made me feel as I did about her . . .

One day in late May, just before the breeding season, Joan was standing motionless in a rainforest near Mission Beach. She was watching with total fascination a female cassowary foraging in the undergrowth. Because conditions were wet, she was wearing rubber gumboots.

For Joan Bentrupper Baumer these were the best times of all: when she and Mother Nature met face to face in a particularly lovely part of the world.

Suddenly, Joan was aware of something shuffling near her feet.

A black-and-white piglet!

How on earth it had gotten there without her being aware of it she had no real idea.

Within a matter of moments, more piglets appeared, until they were all around her—ten, eleven, a dozen. Some of them tried to scamble up her rubber-covered lower legs, standing on their hindfeet, and their circus-like antics when they were unable to almost made Joan burst out laughing.

Then, as though tiring of her, the piglets *en masse* made a direct beeline for the cassowary. They also milled about her feet and, again, some of them tried without success to climb up her scaly legs. Fortunately for the piglets the bird, which could have quite easily trampled or kicked them to death, was a good-tempered sort, which cannot be said of all cassowaries, and, instead of aggression, she simply walked away from the annoying little pigs after a few minutes.

The piglets, Joan had added, were all the same two-toned colour; apparently black and white pigs are common in this part of Queensland. They were also identical in size and were, she'd thought, of the same litter.

'Twelve, you said?'

'Yes, twelve.'

'A big litter,' I said, stating the obvious.

Joan Bentrupper Baumer smiled a particularly nice smile and said, 'They're producing very well around here.'

I wonder why I was rather pleased about that.

7 In Crocodile Habitat

Daly River, Northern Territory

Motionless, the saltwater crocodile lay mostly hidden in lush green growth near the river's western bank. It might have been the solid, gnarled trunk of a tree swept down from a rain-lashed hinterland when raging floodwaters turned the now placid waterway into a potential deathtrap for mounted stockman or domestic beast.

So very little of the crocodile could be seen even when you were close to it, which we were. The eyes were visible of course. Crocodile eyes. Even in broad daylight—when the pupils resembled thin slits—those eyes were all seeing. At night the pupils enlarged dramatically, like those of an owl, and like a bird of the night its night vision was superb. So day or night there was very little—if indeed anything of significance—that such a crocodile as this—by sight and sense—would not be aware of in its territory: a pig, agile wallaby, cattle beast or horse, or even an Aboriginal woman who filled a container with water at a certain place, and at a particular time each day, might be watched very carefully, even surreptitiously, for several days or even weeks. The crocodile might plan an ambush, to lie in wait, mostly hidden, and then with blinding, mind-freezing speed to strike. And if it wasn't inclined to act at the present time, then it might subconsciously note for possible further use precisely when and where that particular food source was.

Now, crouched in the bow of a runabout with its outboard motor switched off, I half-turned and keeping an eye on the crocodile beckoned with short, sharp gestures of urgency for my two companions—Michael Clarke and his mate—to move closer. They nodded to indicate they had understood my gesture and dipped an oar apiece into the water with a soft plip-plopping, plip-plopping sound. Closer and still closer we went towards the all-seeing eyes of the crocodile.

And still the crocodile remained there; it was as though it didn't really think we could see it. Again I gestured and I sensed rather than heard Michael's sharp intake of breath as they slowly uplifted their oars and the front of the boat nudged rather gently into the springy growth that formed a narrow belt and mostly concealed the crocodile.

'Close enough!' hissed Michael.

I nodded in agreement. Close enough was too close really, for had it been so inclined, that crocodile with one almighty leap could have joined us in the runabout. But I was counting on it acting in a predictable fashion, which isn't very sensible when you're dealing with a scaly throwback to the age of the dinosaur, and so when it lunged away from us and cleared the river growth and then slipped under the water with barely a ripple it was in effect doing what perhaps 999 out of 1000 saltwater crocodiles will do in a similar set of circumstances. The problem is the one that doesn't perform according to plan.

'Big one,' said Michael. He pulled a face. 'Don't like getting that close to them.'

'Me neither,' admitted his mate.

'C'mon,' I said. 'Let's go find another croc to photograph.'

My companions looked at each other without revealing just what was on their minds. Perhaps it was just as well that I didn't know.

Northern Territory Museum of Arts and Sciences Darwin,
A few days previously

Genial Dr Max King, a bearded and burly 47-year-old, was in a most expansive mood as we faced each other in his well-appointed office. The curator of terrestrial vertebrates in one of Darwin's most interesting places to visit was talking about a pet subject—hunting, and, with very little prompting on my part, a certain predator of feral pigs in the Top End. The saltwater crocodile.

In 1990, Max says, a good mate of his, Graeme Sawyer, was hunting pigs in the Swim Creek Fauna Reserve: an expansive swamp system looked after by the local conservation commission which, from time to time, let responsible hunters have a crack at the abundant pig population.

Presently, Sawyer had stumbled across a well-used gametrail—pigs obviously. The more he followed the trail, the more churned up and boggy it became. The trail entered a shallow pool of water and beyond it continued on into dense forest. The surrounds of the pool, the hunter noted, were chopped up by the passage of untold numbers of hard-rimmed hoofs. Scattered through the upturned earth were bones. Pig bones. The place might have been a burial ground for *Sus scrofa*. Odd?

As Sawyer went to bypass the water, to avoid getting his feet wet, he suddenly noticed, and much to his surprise, the exposed head and partly submerged body of a crocodile. How on earth he had failed to observe it until now he would never know! Holding his breath, he recognised the beast for a male and judged its length at—what?—12 feet. Not too big, then, but plenty big enough when push turns to shove.

Hey! There was another crocodile here, too. A female. She was smaller than the male. The crocodiles were facing in opposite directions, so that both approaches to the watering place were covered. Yes, they were waiting with untold patience for whatever animal or bird would blunder into their trap. Again, Sawyer's eyes swept over the pig bones. Now he knew why they were here, didn't he?

The crocodiles were unmoving, like wooden carvings in a New Guinea village. Looking at them now, Sawyer realised with disgust that he didn't have his camera with him. What a wasted opportunity! But perhaps with luck they would still be here at this place of ambush tomorrow.

So next day, with a view to photographing these crocodiles, and accompanied by Max King and two others, Sawyer returned to the same spot. Upon reaching it, his fears that the crocodiles would be gone were fully justified.

But where had they gone? the men wondered aloud. This after all was the dry season and water

was scarce. Sure, crocs could travel between water, often covering a fair distance, invariably overnight lest the sun sizzled their brains and killed them by dehydration.

But the men did not speculate about where the crocodiles had gone for too long because the pool of water was linked to a freshwater spring about 100 metres away by two round-bottomed slideways. At the edge of the freshwater spring there were the footmarks and skidmarks of two different crocodiles—both sets of prints fresh—and they presumed the crocodiles were at the bottom of the spring, hiding.

What was unusual about all this, Max Kings says, is that the crocodiles appeared to have made a conscious decision that one area—that is, the pool on the well-used trail—was for hunting purposes and the larger and much deeper spring served as a refuge.

Well, I had listened to all this, finding it fascinating stuff. It made me recall something about the alligator/pig relationship in Nicaragua and how the alligators prey on pigs there. It appears the alligators, taking full advantage of the fact that pigs need water to drink or mud in which to wallow, often half-bury themselves in mud near a river's edge and there they wait—as motionless as the crocodile I observed down the Daly—for pigs to arrive. Once they have seized their prey—usually piglets or half-grown animals—the alligators return with haste to water where they invariably drown their prey or, like a bigger saltwater crocodile, quite literally shake it to bits, limb from limb, head from torso.

But now, facing Max King in Darwin, I mulled over what he had just told me and put the question, might not what they had seen be a one-off situation?

'Definitely not!' Max came back, shaking his head emphatically and then explained that the hunting/refuge network they had found in 1990 was corroborated a year later when they discovered several of these linking networks on the fringes of a rainforest.

'You mean in the same general area, Max?'

'They were about five kilometres from the first one we found,' Max replied, adding that in this case too the pools were used as hunting areas and were connected by water-filled slideways to refuge holes deep within rainforest thickets. In short, the location of the hunting area—the only water available to drink in a large area—meant that the crocodiles were lying in wait for whatever came in from the dry scrubland to the edge of the rainforest to drink. And there, Max finished, they would remain and feed opportunistically until the return of the wet season brought with it a renewal of their swamp system habitat.

So with crocodiles preying on pigs, a logical question is what if any impact do feral pigs have on the crocodile population? Obviously such an opportunistic feeder as a feral pig will take crocodile eggs if a nest site is unprotected. But that, presumably, is rare.

To find out more on this aspect of the feral pig/saltwater crocodile situation in the Top End I had a yarn with Brett Ottley, who is a field assistant to Dr Grahame Webb, considered the Northern Territory's crocodile expert. At the time, Webb was working for a private company (on contract to the local Conservation Commission) on saltwater crocodile research.

Using a helicopter for ease of access, Webb and Ottley visit as many as 200 crocodile nests a year; one year they checked out 250 nests. The country they cover is all prime pig habitat. Only twice, Brett says, has he seen evidence to suggest that pigs have molested a nest site. In both instances there were rotten eggs in the immediate vicinity of the nest and that suggested to Brett that the nest had been flooded and consequently abandoned by the female.

According to Dr Grahame Webb: 'In the wild, saltwater crocodile eggs suffer a very high mortality. In some tidal river systems, widespread flooding occurs with the heavy rains of the wet season, and over 90 per cent of the nests on the river banks are submerged. Embryos need to 'breathe' through the eggshell and shell membrane, and drown if the eggs are submerged.'

In Grahame Webb's opinion, 'Feral pigs are thought to raid nests with viable eggs in parts of Queensland, but no such instances are known in the Northern Territory.'

The main reason Grahame Webb believes that feral pig predation of crocodile eggs does not take place in the Top End is because of the female of the species. She remains at, or close to, the nest site for the entire incubation period, about three months. There is no real need for her to move away from it, because she can survive on very little—if any—food for long periods. At this particular time, then, her sole mission in life is to protect her unborn young contained in eggs buried deep under rotting vegetation, which given sufficient time generates enough heat to incubate them.

At this period a female crocodile is aggression itself. On occasions, as Brett Ottley has witnessed, she will not retreat from on top of the nest even when a helicopter is hovering just above it, its rotor blades causing a wicked downdraught, its engine creating what to a wild creature must be a terrifying sound. She may if suitably aroused fling herself bodily at such a helicopter, as if, by grasping it with her jaws, she can vanquish it—a magnificent gesture. Again, there are several known instances in the Top End when men have been attacked by nesting saltwater crocodiles because they ventured either deliberately or unintentionally too close to a nest site. So it would be a very foolish pig indeed that would dare to approach—let alone start to dig up—the nest of a crocodile containing viable eggs should the female of the species be on guard duty.

From my own research into feral pig predation of crocodile eggs it would seem as though the less aggressive and considerably smaller freshwater species, which nests in the same manner, is definitely at some risk. In Lakefield National Park and several other locations on Cape York Peninsula, pigs have been observed unearthing the nests of freshwater crocodiles to feed on viable eggs.

8 An Island Situation

In a dried-up billabong on Bathurst Island Greg 'Hunter' Freney paused and made a rather dramatic sweeping motion with the back of a hand, explaining that just a month ago the billabong had been extensively covered with tall reed grass—a sea of green which pigs had dug up industriously to get at the tasty bulbous roots.

'Looks like it's all been cultivated by man, doesn't it?' he said, 'but it's all the work of pigs.'

Hard-working legions of pigs, I thought, as I looked about me: the billabong was long and narrow, and the digging very much resembled a linked network of grenade craters where regular nighttime warfare was still going on. For instance, in some of the smooth, clayey bottoms of the holes (very moist) were the rounded indentations of probing snouts. A large, fresh hoofmark at the edge of one such excavation drew my attention.

'Hey, look at this!'

Husky Hunter joined me and considered the spoor.

'Big pig, all right,' he said, cradling in gentle hands an extra-long barrelled US-made .45 calibre blackpowder rifle, based on the famous Hawken of the 1880s. The heavy firearm would come in real handy, I thought, if for one reason or another the mechanism failed to ignite the charge: you could then quite literally beat a nasty boar about the head with it providing you had the same powerful, bear-like frame of Hunter and his devil-may-care attitude to go with the physique.

Why Hunter?

Well, he'd been nicknamed that ever since he was seven years old, at which time he had taken up a single-shot .22 rifle and gone deerstalking on the family property in southern Queensland. All on his own he had shot a fine 14-point red stag. Greg 'Hunter Freney' had been hunting regularly ever since that memorable day 34 years ago.

Apart from the rifle he cradled, he was armed by way of a Smith & Wesson .357 handgun. It was at his waistbelt in a holster and, in case you're wondering, he did have a licence to use it. The piece had such a snub-nosed barrel you'd be pushed to nail a pig at ten paces with it, and, when I said as much to Hunter, he'd grinned and said, a bit further than that, he reckoned.

In any event, he was dressed in faded safari-type clothing, was sporting a bushy beard, and, taking into account the odd combination of firearms, he came across to me as a mixture of Daniel Boone and a highway patrolman out of Dallas. But Hunter was of course a dinky-di Aussie.

The hunter and I pressed on, into the floodplain forest. It was a top day. Presently, Hunter stopped next to a variety of pandanus tree or palm. He touched a big cluster of fruit which, given sufficient time to ripen, would fall to earth.

'Pigs love the stuff,' Hunter said. 'Abo tucker, too.' A pause. 'A lot of the fruit falls down when the fires go through here.' The fires were made by local Aborigines. Indeed, the low-lying island about 80 kilometres northwest of Darwin had been heavily smudged with the smoke of man-made fires when I'd arrived here by air late yesterday afternoon. 'The Tiwi do a lot of burning-off this time of the year,' Hunter added for good measure. In local idiom Tiwi meant 'We People'. The name Tiwi Islands links Bathurst and neighboring Melville Island in a collective group.

Ready for a spell, but more likely a smoke, Hunter hunkered down and fished into his shirt pocket for a packet of cigarettes.

'That big hoofmark back yonder,' I said. 'What size do they grow to here?'

Hunter lighted up. 'Well, in the year that I've been here I've seen a lot of boars that'd go two-fifty, three hundred pounds. Big enough for you?'

'Big enough for anybody.'

'Right,' agreed the man with 20 years of hard-won experience relating to pigs behind him. He drew deeply on the weed, looked thoughtful. 'Oddly enough, there seem to be three different types of pigs on the island . . . '

Hunter went on: the really big boars he'd told me about were all pitch black in colour, they were an almost razorback type of pig with short snouts. He considered they were of British origin.

The second variety of pig he'd observed was also black but was a decidedly smaller animal with a very long snout. The long snout, he believed, hinted very strongly at an Asian influence.

'I mean, we're only 180 miles from Timor here,' he pointed out, 'aren't we? What's that? Sea traders could've easily put some ashore long ago.' True enough, they could have.

Lastly, Hunter said, he had often encountered a medium-sized pig that may be ginger, ginger/white, ginger/black, or black-and-white, and once he'd seen a saddleback pig.

'Saddleback, huh,' I said. 'Where did that one come from, eh?'

The fishing guide grinned through his beard.

'Buggered if I know, mate,' Hunter said. 'Buffalo's been here much longer'n me—reckon he'll fill you in on a few things about pigs.

Bara Base Lodge on Bathurst Island is owned by the Tiwi people. It is a well organised setup on the beachfront that caters basically for those who want to catch the far north's number-one game fish: barramundi. The fishing is not just good at Bara Base—it is superb!

Wayne 'Buffalo' Ross is the manager of Bara Base, a position he has held for eight years. He is built on the lines of an undersized Japanese sumo wrestler, hence, I suppose, the nickname.

At the lodge, Buffalo slurped on a can of beer.

'Pigs? No, mate, there weren't any here in the early days according to the Tiwi—what we've got here really started in the early sixties . . . '

By all accounts there was a considerable pig farm on the island in early 1963, located in the southeast corner, where most of the population (about 1000 people) lived. The pig farm came to an end later that year when overnight the pigs, *en masse,* breached the fences and raced off, perhaps with piggy squeals of glee. How many pigs were involved here? Buffalo didn't know the exact figure but said he'd been told

by a local it was 'big mobs of pigs' and in Aboriginal lingo that always signified a large number of animals. A few pigs had apparently been recaptured or may have willingly surrendered. But as for the rest, well, an 2000 square kilometre paradise was there for the taking. And take it the ex-domesticated pigs did.

Overall, Bathurst Island is about a third the size of Melville Island. Habitat consists of extensive savannah woodlands, huge swamps and even tropical jungle. Freshwater springs abound. No one has yet tried to estimate the feral pig population here and perhaps like elsewhere that would be a hopeless task. According to Wayne Ross, there had been a huge increase in their numbers in the time he had been here. They were often seen in mobs 25–30 strong, the boars grew trophy-sized tusks, and they were presently found all over the island.

Hunting pressure? That was light. The Tiwi much prefer to hunt wallaby, Buffalo said, and used 12-gauge shotguns rather than traditional spears. A few Europeans living on the island chased them with dogs. No one bothered to look for them where there wasn't road (track) access.

'They've got it pretty easy really,' Buffalo summed up.

So with pigs widespread on Bathurst Island, a logical question is why aren't there any on Melville Island. Remember, there were pigs there in 1826— 54 of them by all accounts. Pigs from the south, most likely: domestic breeds. As already said, the likely explanation as to what happened to these pigs is that they were deliberately left behind, or may have been existing in a semi-feral state, when Fort Dundas was given up as a bad job in 1827. That being the case, then why didn't they survive there? Like Bathurst Island, Melville Island it too offers all that a feral pig could want in the way of habitat and food. Perhaps those pigs—most likely rather tame at that stage— were quickly killed off by the locals with clubs and spears. Who really knows?

Today, there are two reasons why pigs are not found on Melville Island: no one has bothered to liberate them there, and a stretch of water naturally separates the two islands. This is called Lord Apsleys Strait, named by Philip Parker King who surveyed and named both islands in 1818–19. As a matter of interest, Bathurst Island was named after the colonial secretary at that particular time.

At any rate, Lord Apsleys Strait is very nearly 73 kilometres in length. Typical of far northern waters,

The lovely Daly River.

Saltwater crocodile in hiding on the Daly River, positioned so it could easily ambush animals, including pigs, when they came to water.

While it is obviously small, this waterhole could in the dry season contain a full-grown saltwater crocodile, and is an ideal place for one to wait until prey arrives . . .

Pig predation of crocodile eggs is thought to be slight. In Lakefield National Park, where it does sometimes happen, Graham Hardwicke examines the nest of a saltwater crocodile possibly damaged by flooding.

Greg 'Hunter' Freney striding across a sunbaked billabong where pig rooting is extensive.

The fruit of the pandanus palm is sought after by foraging pigs.

Above: Dingoes prey heavily on piglets and young and/or sick animals. Undoubtedly they are the number one predators of pigs in Australia.

Left: Jim Thompson (standing) and Brett McCahon checking out pig damage in Lakefield National Park.

Below: There is a wide variety of habitat for wild pigs on Bathurst Island. Pigs are often seen from the air in the open country which in the wet season is under water.

a 7.5-metre tide rips through this comparatively narrow channel, the currents are vicious, the many whirlpools deadly. Moreover, saltwater crocodiles patrol these formidable waters, as do sharks of various types, mostly tiger and hammer-head. A number of Tiwi people have lost their lives in the dangerous waters of Lord Apsleys Strait, and we may presume, with confidence I feel, that the same fate has befallen some pigs too.

'Having said that,' said Wayne 'Buffalo' Ross, still on the subject of why there weren't any pigs on Melville Island, 'one of our guides reckoned he saw some there a couple of years ago.' Now wasn't that interesting?

The fishing guide in question was Lance Butler and from what he said he'd observed several pigs— little more than a fleeting glimpse—in the vicinity of Goose Creek, located in the far north of the island. That was in 1991. Butler made no secret of what he had seen and pretty soon the super-sensitive ears of the local Conservation Commission pricked up. Pigs on Melville Island? Struth, that was as bad as the Japs bombing Darwin all over again!

Buffalo chuckled.

'So they chartered a chopper and checked out the area where Lance said he'd seen them, but they didn't find any there or, for that matter, any sign, either.' He fingered his dark beard thoughtfully. 'Really, I hope Lance was mistaken—pigs've caused enough problems here without them starting the same thing across the Strait.'

It was my turn to look thoughtful. 'But you don't think he was mistaken, do you . . . ?'

The huge Buffalo, slumped in a chair in the bar-cum-dining room, shook his bullet-like head from side to side:

'No, I don't . . . y'see, Lance isn't the type to say he saw a pig when he didn't.' He paused and, putting down a can of beer, spread both hands wide. 'And just because the Conservation boys didn't get onto any . . . '

Like I said earlier, Melville Island is three times the size of Bathurst and the latter covers about 2000 square kilometres. On Melville Island there are places, deep in swamps, where no one sensibly goes. There could be crocodiles a century old in there. Could be pigs breeding up, exploding in numbers, and no one would even know it.

I was on my second beer now, enjoying it too.

'You said something about pig damage here,

Buffalo. What sort of damage did you mean?'

'You've already seen a heap of rooting with Hunter?'

'True.'

'Well, it's really bad in some parts of the island. I could show you places where they've really stuffed things up.'

'In what way?'

Buffalo explained that by extensive rooting on the beaches and adjacent country they had in a number of places created channels whereby saltwater was able to penetrate freshwater billabongs.

'That buggers up the whole ecology,' Buffalo summed up succinctly.

I finished my beer and told Buffalo I was going for a walk along the beach before dinner.

'Watch out for crocs,' he warned.

'Count on it, mate!' I retorted flatly.

I retired to my room at Bara Base Lodge early that night. The guest rooms more or less overlook the beach. At night, as a safety measure against crocodiles, powerful spotlights illuminate the beachfront area. Crocodiles? Buffalo told me that no one is allowed to walk on the beaches at night here and, by shining a powerful torch, you could oftentimes see their red eyes just out there in front of the lodge.

Just three years ago a pet dog, a blue heeler, had spotted a really big crocodile during the daylight cruising about 10 metres offshore. Typically, it had rushed to the water's edge and barked frantically, all its attention riveted on the crocodile, now more or less motionless. The very bottom line is that this crocodile was bait and another crocodile, only a few metres offshore, was waiting in ambush with only its eyes showing above the water level. Jaws gaping, it exploded out of the water like an express train thundering out of a tunnel. Whump! A bite-size dog is top tucker where a crocodile is concerned.

Tonight, within radius of the spotlight's beam, the sea was black and smooth and appeared most sinister because you knew for a fact there were some really big crocodiles out there and that any one of them, given the opportunity, would most likely take you in its incredibly powerful jaws and quite literally shake you limb from limb. Yes, just out there, in the water, waiting, watching . . .

And of course pigs would be up and about too. Some of them living in close proximity to the sea would wander onto the beaches and shallows in search of food. The Tiwi people eat well on crabs, mussels and, in season, turtle eggs. Pigs too enjoy this kind of seafood. They also eat carrion washed ashore. Yes, our *Sus scrofa* does very well for itself on Bathurst, and, indeed, other islands where it can be found off the coast of the Northern Territory.

Today, there are well-established colonies of feral pigs on Croker, Peron, the Goulbourns, and Elcho Island. Talking of Elcho Island, the following little story appeared in the *Sunday Territorian* of 8 November 1985:

Man's best friend a pig?

A big, black hairy pig is hardly anyone's idea of an ideal pet but Marrdakani is just that.

She wandered into Djurranaldi outstation on Elcho Island, about 500 km east of Darwin, more than12 months ago, and stayed.

Beautiful she is not but there is no danger of this pig going into the pot. The small Aboriginal community which has adopted her and obviously feeds her well, describes Marrdakani as a 'decoration' and treats her as the family pet.

'Sometimes she goes with us to the beach and has a swim with us,' one of the community, Jenny Wulumdhuna, said.

'She also has a son,' Jenny said. Sure enough, a second look revealed a cute piglet with ginger stripes, and it was hard to imagine Marrdakani once was as small as that.

My all too short visit to Bathurst Island was about to come to an end one sunny Saturday evening as I waited at the airstrip (reached by boat from the lodge) with Hunter and some outward-bound fishing types wearing suntans you'd never get in Melbourne this time of the year. Back to Darwin then—the Top End's lackadaisical version of the Big Smoke.

Hunter smoked while we waited for the Cessna 210 to turn up. I had been in his company for much of my time on the island. He was one of those larger than real life characters you're more likely to meet well off the beaten track than in a city.

For his part, Hunter was very disappointed that we hadn't seen a pig on the island. Knowing how he'd felt, I'd shrugged it off and said, well, we had seen a lot of signs, which certainly proved something, and the varied habitat had been interesting and after all there were no guarantees when you're dealing with wildlife, whatever the species, and Hunter had nodded

philosophically at that and said, yeah, I was dead right there.

Presently the Cessna came into view, banked around the head of the airstrip and came down. It taxied towards us.

The pilot was the same one who had flown me in here. Brett Carter was blond-haired, a rather smooth-looking type enjoying life in the Top End.

'Pigs?' Brett had said the first time around. 'Yeah, we often see them when we're coming in to land on the island. Keep an eye open on a big swamp near the landing strip, okay?' On my initial flight, however, the pigs hadn't revealed themselves.

Hunter extended a hard hand and said, 'Pity it was so short, Phil.'

I nodded in agreement and said those were my feelings too.

'Maybe next time, huh?' Hunter proved he had a bone-crushing handshake.

'Hey, who knows.'

At the end of the runway the Cessna turned about and, picking up speed, soon gained enough momentum to lift off the ground. I observed where pigs had rooted up the open ground between the airstrip and the forest. The diminutive figure of Hunter raised a hand as we swept over him. Long way from a property in southern Queensland, wasn't it, Hunter?

Only from the air was it really possible to gauge the size of Bathurst Island. Also, it was all low-lying, there wasn't a decent hillock in sight. Nor did there appear to be any open country as such. Rather, it was all forest, swamps, winding ribbons of water.

There were untold numbers of pigs down there, wide-ranging descendants of the animals which took to the wild more than 30 years ago. They were truly feral now, both in appearance and outlook. How many they had mushroomed to was of course anyone's guess. Given the size of the island, an educated guess would put their numbers in the thousands. Most certainly there were enough of them to make commercial hunting a viable proposition, as well as a sensible one. The fact they were judged TB free was a big incentive to capatalise on them.

But for the present there wasn't any significant hunting on Bathurst Island and the saltwater crocodiles and dingoes most likely accounted for many more than man did.

To the north, I saw a winding silver stretch of water very nearly 73 kilometres in length. This evening, Lord Apsleys Strait appeared deceptively calm.

Beyond this channel of water was of course Melville Island, an important link in the story of the wild pig in Australia. I'd been told by Wayne 'Buffalo' Ross that there was a herd of water buffalo on Melville Island estimated to be 5000 strong. Many of the bulls were reputed to carry magnificent horns, top trophies. Melville Island? Now wouldn't that be a wonderful place to visit, to explore at length. And who knows— maybe, just maybe—you'd come across some familiar rooting near a swamp or wherever and you'd realise with a start that Bathurst Island wasn't the only landmass in the Tiwi group inhabited by wild pigs.

9 Cape York Peninsula: Stronghold of the Wild Pig

Bizant Outstation, Lakefield National Park, Cape York Peninsula

At 5.20 am a dingo howled and I was instantly wide awake as I lay in my comfortable swag on the hard wooden floor of one of the outstation's several bedrooms.

I mulled over the incident with the charging black boar that Brett McCahon and John McManus couldn't wait to tell everyone about when they had arrived here yesterday evening. I thought, too, about where I was and the wild pigs that ranged here in their many, many thousands. What? Right, an estimated 20 000 of them. Also, there was one of the largest concentrations of saltwater crocodiles in the park, and so many species of birds. What a truly fantastic place Lakefield National Park really was.

Before the Queensland National Parks and Wildlife Service had purchased the land in 1979 there had been a cattle station here—rated as one of the best on Cape York Peninsula. The cattle station had known a number of owners in its colourful 98-year history. Before then the land was a prime hunting ground for Aborigines, and naturally enough they had no fond feelings whatsoever for those early white settlers who took up land north of Cairns.

While records are at best sketchy about this particular place at this particular time it does appear as though a teamster called Donald McKenzie took up what became known as Lakefield station in 1881. The Scotsman ran cattle, built a rough homestead, planted and cultivated a garden. At any rate, McKenzie was in his garden one day when the local blacks—to make a pertinent point about land ownership—speared him to death.

In 1908 the station was taken on by the O'Beirne family—two brothers by all accounts—of adjacent Laura station (now within the boundaries of Lakefield National Park). Later, they sold both stations as a combined run to Brian and Pat Grogan, who now had 9000 square kilometres at their disposal.

A man called Charlie Wallace held title to the station in the 1950s and in 1966 the Tipperary Land Company of America gained control of the huge property. The Americans sold out in 1978 to a partnership from New South Wales and a year later they relinquished the rights to the Queensland NPWS.

During my stay in the park, I was fortunate enough to meet the ranger in charge here. His name was Ron Teece and he just happened to have been the manager of Lakefield station from 1974 until it became a national park five years later.

At Bizant Outstation Ron and I yarned in the sun, Ron hunkered down like a stockman with his back propped comfortably against a tree, busy with a packet of smokes.

Ron Teece was in his fifties—on the low side of 55, at a guess. He was a lean, greying weatherworn type wearing a brown Akubra hat with a high crown, a tan service-issue shirt, brown R.M. Williams riding pants, and flat-heeled, elastic-sided suede boots. He looked like he'd been up a thousand dry creekbeds and over the same number of red sandhills. And by his clothing, which suited him very well, it was rather difficult to fathom out if he was really on the National Park's payroll or whether he still figured he was cracking the stockwhip on a station that had ceased to exist 14 years ago.

'We had a crew of about twenty here then,' Ron drawled. 'There was the main station headquarters—

Lakefield—where I still live. You must've seen that on your way in here?'

'Uh-huh,' I confirmed. 'We ran two outstations,' Ron continued. 'Here at Bizant and New Laura . . . yeah . . . ' He appeared reflective as he pulled deeply on his smoke, his eyes all crinkled up in the corners, those dry creekbeds awfully close.

'Cattle? Oh, we had about twelve thousands on the books—all sorts of breeds; you name it, we had it. There was a lot of feral cattle here, too. Still is as a matter of fact. How many? At least a thousand, I'd say. Course they can be awful hard to spot on a place this size . . . ' Ron permitted himself the ghost of a smile.

'Pigs? My word, yes! There was even more then than there are today, I reckon. We used to write off about eight per cent of the cattle to death by natural causes, so that was a major supply of food for them. When the cattle went, well, the pig had to turn pretty much vegetarians.' He ashed his cigarette. 'No worries there, eh?'

Presently, Ron Teece straightened—a few kinks there, I'd say. He said he'd see me later and ambled off with a cowman's gait to find his transport. I half expected to see him take off on a horse but he had a four-wheel-drive vehicle instead.

Once again a dingo howled in the early hours at Bizant Outstation—that is, about 5.45, early to some.

'Noisy bastard!' Graham Hardwicke grunted from the depths of his insect-proof swag—a cocoon-like affair not designed for claustrophobics but ideal if you happened to be bedding down for the night next to an insect-ridden swamp. 'Getting a bloody good feed of iodine into it, I expect,' Graham added. He was most likely right there: an uncovered trailer-load of already prepared pigbaits was about 30 metres from where we were sharing a bedroom, Fortunately the wind was blowing in the right direction! Smell? Up close it was enough to knock you over, enough for a dingo three rivers away to get the message that, hey, Bizant Outstation was the right place to be.

Again the dingo cried out; distantly came a reply.

Then some brolgas started carrying on in the scrub—a strange trumpeting racket.

'Jeez!' Graham complained, 'how does a man get any sleep around here?'

'You're supposed to have already had it.

'Suppose so.' He yawned. 'Maybe I should get up and make a cuppa tea . . . '

'Good idea. You know How I like it—not too strong, milk, no sugar.'

So Graham unzipped his swag—a very loud tearing sound which hadn't done a thing for me in the middle of the night when he'd answered nature's urgent call—and stood up with a shiver. While it was far from cold, we must be considerate and remember that Queensland winters are cold to locals.

From the next bedroom, Jim Mitchell called out: 'What time is it?'

Graham squinted at his wristwatch in the poor light.

'Six o'clock.'

'Suppose that was you howling . . . wasn't it?'

Graham paused in the doorway of the next bedroom and, tossing back his head, made a dingo-like call.

'Told you there was far too much curry in that stew you made last night, mate!' Jim fired back.

All typical good-natured banter with the Rural Lands Protection Board boys.

Graham was pouring tea into tin mugs when I joined him in the roomy kitchen-cum-dining area. Steaming mug in hand I went outside to savour at length the first brew of the day and also to soak up the start of another brand-new morning north of the Tropic of Capricorn.

There was real warmth in the air now; later the temperature would perhaps nudge 35 degrees, but it was a lovely dry heat consistent with the season.

You know, I had really landed on my feet by being allowed to come here with the government boys to Lakefield National Park on—of all things—a feral pig project. I mean, how fortunate could I really get: the time I had planned to spend in north Queensland had coincided with this particular venture and Graham Hardwicke had gone right out of his way in gaining permission (from Jim Mitchell) for me to accompany them.

Moreover, each of the four Queenslanders had had a lot to do with feral pigs and was only too willing to talk about his experiences—not that it had taken much prompting, you understand, for John and Brett to breathlessly explain about the boar attacking them for, on the surface, no good reason at all.

Living at Charters Towers, John McManus and Brett McCahon didn't have to travel too far to find feral pigs—pigs, in fact, resided very close to town.

At the present time, John said, a huge black boar the locals had named Homer was ranging station country fringing Charters Towers. Homer was estimated to be about 130 kg on the hoof. The black boar had earned itself quite a reputation for being both an elusive and dangerous animal. He had been hunted deliberately many times without success, and he'd not only roughed up a few dogs but had also killed several that John knew of.

Just four weeks previously—June, 1993—John and Brett had linked forces in an attempt to put down Homer once and for all.

They used two dogs on the day in question—big, powerful dogs. Chopper was a bull mastiff cross with a huge chest, and Boof was a boxer cross. Only Boof was fitted out with a leather chest shield. This turned out to be a mistake because—in their short but savage encounter with Homer—Boff was only lightly wounded but Chopper was badly cut by 12-centimetre gashes across his chest and shoulders.

'We'll get him one of these days,' John finished. 'No worries.'

Well, I guess big Homer had his own ideas about that, right?

In retrospect, I'd have to rate Jim Mitchell as the most knowledgeable person on pigs I met during the fieldwork for this book; certainly his understanding of feral pigs in the Queen state is unsurpassed.

Over a 12-year period, Jim Mitchell's research and control work on feral pigs has taken him to Moreton Island—a national park near Brisbane, out west on the South Australian border, to Aborigine reserves near the tip of Cape York Peninsula, and just about everywhere else you can find pigs in Queensland.

'Moreton Island?' I asked.

Jim Mitchell raised his eyebrows and pulled a disgusted face:

'Listen, we took 200 pigs off there in 1983–84 and reckoned there were about a dozen or so left in a swamp at the south end of the island. We then handed the responsibility of pig control back to the National Parks but they didn't do anything about it and now there's pigs all over the island!'

'A lot of work for nothing then?'

'Yeah—something like that.'

I was intrigued that Jim had seen pigs so far out west, for surely pigs living out on the border with South Australia were inhabiting desert country.

'Too right they are,' Jim agreed. 'It's mostly sandhills out there.'

'So what are they living on?

'Air and rocks, I guess.' Jim laughed. 'Seriously, I think they live on underground tubers and lizards and snakes.' He shrugged. 'Whatever they can find, I reckon.'

'What sort of condition were they in?'

'Pretty good nick,' Jim replied. He then added that he'd only seen boars out there, and that they were normally on their own. 'Funny the places boars turn up, isn't it?'

In 1981–82, Jim Mitchell and some others did a survey on pig numbers and their distribution—shire by shire—in Queensland. They came to the conclusion that 60 per cent of feral pigs could be found north of a line between Townsville and Mount Isa, with by far the greatest numbers here on Cape York Peninsula.

There are very nearly 50 cattle stations on Cape York Peninsula and pigs, in varying numbers, ranging from low to heavy, are found on every single one of them.

Perhaps the greatest concentrations of pigs at the present time north of Cairns can be found in Aurukun Aboriginal Reserve—located on the crocodile-infested Archer River south of Weipa.

No pig control work goes on here and Aborigines have never regarded wild pig highly as a food source. Also, the area requires a hunting permit for anyone but an Aborigine, and they are not easy to come by. Consequently hunting pressure is very much on the low side and the pigs, most of them in Lakefield National Park, are rather quiet.

Barry Toms, Jim Mitchell said, was a regional inspector with the department for a dozen years. He knew the Cape as well as anyone did. In the Aboriginal reserve in question, Toms once observed, and photographed, a mob of pigs he estimated at 700 strong.

When Brett McCahon and a mate, Keith Venables, were fortunate enough to gain access to Aurukun Aboriginal Reserve in 1986 on a combined hunting/fishing trip, they were quite staggered by the overwhelming number of pigs they saw there—the vast green floodplains were literally dotted for as far as they could see with thousands of black dots.

'We gave up shooting them after a few days,' Brent recalls. 'There wasn't any real point in killing any more.' After a thoughtful pause, he'd added, 'Never seen pigs like that before or since.'

According to reliable sources, there are still huge mobs of pigs to be seen on this remote Aboriginal land south of the bauxite mining town of Weipa.

And here in Lakefield National Park it is also possible to observe large numbers of feral pigs. By all accounts it is the end of the dry season—October—when they really start to mob up together. By then many months have passed without rain and things are really drying up and the pigs have no other choice but to gather around an ever-diminishing water supply, usually lagoons some distance apart.

So by checking out such watering places in the early morning or late evening you could quite conceivably observe mobs of feral pigs 100, 200, and, in Jim Mitchell's particular case, even 400 strong. But Brent Vincent, a Cairns-based wildlife ranger with the National Parks Service, can go even higher than that.

Brent Vincent's workload revolves mainly around saltwater crocodiles, and Lakefield National Park is contained within his massive area of responsibility, stretching from the Cardwell Shire boundary in the south to around 1.6 kilometres (1 mile) off the New Guinea coastline, including all Cape York Peninsula and the islands of the Torres Strait.

It was November, Brent recalls, when he and a fellow wildlife ranger, Buzz Symonds, arrived at the far, northern boundary of Lakefield National Park, en route to Cairns.

'We'd been up there on a law enforcement run,' Brent explained. 'Looking out for poachers. People operating outside the law . . . Stuff like that.'

'Poaching what?'

'Crocs, mate. Crocs!' Brent had shot back as though that was the dumbest question he'd heard since he'd first worn a ranger's shirt.

They drove into the park. Nearby was a fairly large billabong called Low Lake. From what they'd been told by Ron Teece, Low Lake was so low this year it had actually dried up completely, the first time it had done so in its recorded history. The reason for this was that the previous wet season, for some unknown reason, hadn't been wet at all. But it wasn't a dried-up billabong the two rangers wanted to see; rather, it was a fire that had started burning in the peat at the eastern end of Low Lake some time previously that aroused their curiosity.

'That had to be a phenomenon,' Brent reckoned.

So they clambered out of their Toyota within easy walking distance of Low Lake. Both men were armed, Brent with his own .308 M-77 Ruger carbine, and Buzz using a department issue M-77 Ruger in the same calibre.

'We're always keen to take a few pigs,' said Brent, explaining the firearms. 'That way we can keep our freezer full for croc work.' That is, they bait their traps when they're after troublesome crocodiles—which can mean anything from taking out dogs to far worse crimes—with a lure few big salties can resist.

Slinging his fully-wooded carbine, Brent walked shoulder to shoulder with Buzz as they started through the trees towards Low Lake.

By this time the sun was low, filtering through the trees, and Brent tipped the brim of his hat low over his eyes, the better to see.

There!

Pigs!

Upwind, the pigs, lying down, were unaware of the men. Covered with dust—a dry bath? —they were rather difficult to see.

The men selected a target each and fired.

Suddenly, it seemed as though the entire place was alive with dusty-coated pigs leaping to their feet.

Two more shots rang out, and then two more.

By now the pigs were running, streaming like a great unbroken wave, running into the sun, faster now.

The wildlife rangers stood there in amazement at just what they were witnessing.

A great cloud of dust gathered about the running pigs and it was do dense it obliterated the sun as a partial eclipse had taken place, and the noise of so many hard-rimmed hoofs on the hard ground was like the sound of rolling thunder.

Some time later, as they looked at the fire they had come to see, they could still hear, in the distance, the echoing sound of the pigs still on the move.

Both men considered they had seen somewhere between 500 and 700 feral pigs that day and maybe that was the real phenomenon in Lakefield National Park and not the fire burning in Low Lake . . .

10 The Asian Link

Feral pigs in Australia have more in common with their wild cousins in Eurasia than with domestic pigs. They have similar species classification, genetic constitution, appearance, colour, conformation, behaviour and ecological requirements. To suggest that they are not wild animals and closer to domestic pigs than European wild boar is to ignore available information for reasons not connected with an objective assessment of the animal.

Feral Pigs and Their Distribution, Queensland Rural Lands Protection Board, 1987

One rather overcast evening in Lakefield National Park, I first observed and then spent some time ascertaining the direction of the wind, before attempting to get within close photographic range of an adult black sow feeding on green vegetable matter in a billabong.

Beyond the billabong were a number of piglets—some, I reckoned, belonged to the sow and some to several other sows in the immediate vicinity. All up I was close to about 40 pigs, half of them in the piglet stage. Indeed, the young ones were grouped in a communal fashion, mostly rooting with the unbridled enthusiasm of those to whom such rudimentary acts are second nature.

At any rate, I eventually reached the rather scummy edge of the billabong; the water level was low and it would, I expected, dry up completely within a few weeks.

The sow was long in the leg, and rangy of build. She was also underweight, I thought; a sow invariably loses weight during farrowing and nursing her young.

But it was the shape, or, rather, the length of the sow's head that really arrested my interest: it was just so much longer than the rather blunt-nosed features of pigs of obvious European ancestry. Yes, the Asian origins of this particular pig were unmistakeable; she might, it occurred to me, have

been foraging in a similar lagoon in India or, for that matter, anywhere else *Sus scrofa cristatus* is found.

According to wildlife ranger Brent Vincent, there are feral pigs on all the islands in Princess Charlotte Bay. They are especially concerned about Stanley Island—in the Flinders Group—because it is a National Park.

The largest island falling within Brent's jurisdiction is Prince of Wales Island, formerly Muralug, located off the northwest tip of Cape York Peninsula. There are feral pigs on Prince of Wales Island, and also deer. Rusa deer.

It was because of deer poachers that Brent Vincent went to sort things out in an official capacity. As he explained, all species of deer in Australia are introduced; however, a deer is featured on the Queensland coat of arms and that makes it protected game. Just as well they didn't include a pig there too, I thought.

The deer poachers mostly came from nearby Thursday Island, taking both deer and pigs back with them for wedding and ceremonial feasts. This practice, Brent knows only too well, will never be stamped out completely.

In his book *The Torres Strait*, John Singe says that pigs on Prince of Wales Island are even more abundant than the deer and, in describing them, goes on to write,

The tendency is towards the large-shouldered, savage, black razor backs, though frequently white and black spotted specimens occur. They are probably descendants of Papuan pigs brought down through the islands at some stage. This however is a controversial point. Pigs had definitely been present in southern Papua for a thousand years and were running wild on Saibai in 1873. It therefore seems unlikely that some were not included in the trading between Australia and Papua, yet they never appear in an Island myth or legend. Early Europeans found gardens on Mer guarded by stout fences as if to protect them from a foraging animal such

Freshwater billabong in Lakefield National Park. Saltwater crocodiles inhabit this billabong and wild pigs often wade out to feed on the roots of water lilies, with, presumably, inevitable results.

Ron Teece.

Wildlife ranger Brent Vincent.

Wild pig/saltwater crocodile habitat: Bloomfield River, near Cape Tribulation National Park, Cape York Peninsula.

as a pig, but found no pigs. Perhaps in comparatively recent times they were introduced, found to be too much trouble and all killed. It has been proposed that the pigs on Cape York Peninsula are descendants of those left by Cook, but it is more likely they arrived somehow from Papua.'

The above-mentioned, swamp-ridden Saibai Island lies just 8 kilometres off the Papuan coastline and yet it is still contained within the Queensland border. Saibai is some 24 kilometres in length by 8 kilometres wide. On Saibai, in the period Singe mentions, pigs were both wild and domesticated, a typical situation in this part of the world.

No one knows how long pigs had been on Saibai, but given its close proximity with the huge landmass—Papua—that can be seen from there, it was presumably a very long time. Even so, no pig god—Burumaugadalgal—ever existed on Saibai as, for instance, it did in Papua.

On Saibai the feral pigs played havoc with the unfenced gardens of the villagers who grew, among other tempting foods, taro. Armed with bow and arrow the villagers carried on a relentless war with the pigs and eventually—some time early this century, it is thought—the very last one was killed.

Someone else who believes there is a strong possibility that feral pigs 'may' have been in Australia for longer that 200 years—that is, before European times—is Peter 'Piggy' Pavlov.

Pavlov, a pig ecologist, has studied pigs extensively for 15 years. Interestingly enough, while working on his PhD in pig ecology, he spent a great deal of time in Lakefield National Park. Pavlov chose the wet, rather than dry, season to spend most of his time in the field.

In Lakefield National Park, Pavlov's main area of research was Jane Table Hill, which I observed as a low escarpment between the Bizant and Normanby Rivers. From the summit of Jane Table Hill you can see quite clearly Princess Charlotte Bay. In the wet, Jane Table Hill, the only high ground in a considerable area, becomes a sort of sanctuary for all sorts of wildlife, and Pavlov, often sharing his campsite with snakes, including taipans, did not have to look very hard to observe pigs: they came to him.

More recently, Pavlov has been working with the Wet Tropics Management Authority. In Cape Tribulation, Pavlov reached the intriguing conclusion that pigs in this region are unlike other types anywhere

else in the country, and that they are in fact an entirely different breed, and, accordingly, may well have been here much longer than 200 years.

While Singe's theory that pigs on Cape York Peninsula are more likely of Asian, rather than European, stock can never be proven in a conclusive manner, his hypothesis does merit serious consideration.

The point is this: pigs on Cape York Peninsula—and Peter Pavlov considers the unusual type he has observed to be more of an Asian pig—do in fact resemble pigs from the far east more than what we might term European throwbacks—that is, the wild boar of Europe.

Is it not possible that pigs were on Cape York Peninsula before the white man came to these waters? For one thing, any release made of pigs on Cape York Peninsula would have been almost certainly small. Again, pigs do have a slow dispersal rate during colonisation of an area, and there is no doubt whatever that while they are capable of travelling long distances, the fact they are so widespread in Australia is due largely to man's intervention rather than their own endeavours.

Some interesting information in regard to the 'home range' of feral pigs was gathered by Kim Masters, a postgraduate zoology research student who studied the biology of the species in question in the southwest of Western Australia in the late 1970s and early 1980s.

During this study, a total of 194 pigs were captured in the Kirup, Collie, Harvey, and Owellingup districts. They were tagged and then liberated. Later, 49 of the tagged pigs were recaptured (in traps). None had travelled more than 16 kilometres from where it had originally been caught.

Of these pigs, a boar and two adult sows were retained for further studies: they were fitted with a radio-transmitting collar and then released again. Then for several months they were tracked and monitored using a directional-aerial receiver. These pigs, Masters discovered, had a home range of less than 5 square kilometres.

It must in all fairness be said that pigs in the southern part of Western Australia are almost certainly descended from British domestic stock. Given that is the case, then they may well be more sedentary than their far eastern counterparts which, for the purpose of this excercise, we presume first inhabited Cape York Peninsula.

In his final report to the Conservation Commission of the Northern Territory on feral pigs in the Douglas/Daly river systems, Peter Caley concluded that the home range for boars was 31.2 kilometres, and for sows 19.4 kilometres (boars invariably range much further than sows, most likely due to the mating urge). From his extensive observations Caley considered that the pigs were sedentary and that there was no long-term trend for them to disperse from the study site.

In commenting further on the natural dispersal rate of pigs it is, I think, well worth pointing out that when Timor pigs were left to their own devices with the abandonment of Fort Wellington on the Cobourg Peninsular in 1827 they began a very slow drift to the southwest. So, apparently unaided by man, they were to take about 160 years before they were well established in the Maningridia district of Arnhem Land. As a comparison, a similar release of Asian pigs made at the tip of Cape York Peninsula at the same time would by now have barely extended its range past the Archer River (south of Weipa). By checking out a map, we find this overall distance to be less than half the total length of Cape York Peninsula.

Heavy hunting pressure will naturally accelerate the dispersal of pigs although, in some instances, they may later return to the same area where they were previously harassed.

Also, boars, usually nomadic, will perhaps spearhead the inevitable expansion of the species.

Undeniably, then, there is a very strong Asian influence amongst pigs on Cape York Peninsula: they are in fact very much like those described by John Singe on Prince of Wales Island, which, geographically speaking, is only separated from the Australian mainland by a comparatively narrow passage of water Cook named Endeavour Strait.

The niggling question is when did pigs really arrive on Cape York Peninsula?

11 Observations Afield

Still outstretched on my stomach at the sunbaked edge of the billabong in Lakefield National Park, I took one, two, and then three quick telephoto shots of the unsuspecting black sow foraging on green vegetable matter. I sensed that one of the photographs at least would find a place in this book: the light was good—cloudy bright—and the sow, pausing with snout uplifted as she fed, was in sharp profile.

Later, I would reflect with a somewhat rueful smile on the words that Ida M. Mellen wrote in her book *The Natural History of the Pig*, as I recalled some of the more difficult subjects I'd attempted to photograph other than the black sow during the field research for this particular work.

> Pigs are not photogenic. With snouts to the ground, they turn their heads away from the camera. A good picture of a pig is therefore a triumph in photography.

Meantime, I was, in my peripheral vision, only too aware that a boar was staring intently in my direction. It was a rather calculating expression from under very heavy brows. Typically, he was black: a powerfully built, high-backed animal with visible tusks. Weight? Definitely over 110 kg. Distance from me? About 35–40 metres. As Brett McCahon and John McManus know only too well, a charging boar is indeed fast. How fast? Well, within a matter of a few paces they can attain a speed in excess of 40 km per hour. Taking such a turn of speed into consideration, plus his size and of course those tusks, I considered it prudent to give him my full and undivided attention. Like Brett at the time of the attack, I too was positioned under a tree: a small but solid enough tree with low limbs spreading out in a welcoming fashion. Believe me, one hint of an aggressive move in my direction on that boar's part and those branches just above my head would be embracing me in double-quick time, no worries!

Out in the shallow water, the sow suddenly appeared edgy. At that particular moment an unseen ripple of unease seemed to spread throughout the rest of the pigs there: something was up, all right!

With quick steps and an air of purpose the sow moved out of the billabong and went straight to her brood, which she knew by smell. They congregated about her—five or six, perhaps. They made tiny squealing noises which the sow replied to with much deeper tones. Indeed, it did seem as though all the piglets there—linked up with three sows—were vocal. Add a few squawking hens and a couple of docile sheep to the scene and I might have been standing in a small holding rather than in a national park of immense size. Still, pigs are a most loquacious species.

By this time one of the sows, trailed dutifully by her brood, started away from the far side of the billabong, where she may have been giving them practical lessons in rooting. They walked in no real hurry, but with intent nonetheless, towards a scattered belt of trees fringed by tall grass.

Within a few moments the other pigs went after her, as though, it occurred to me, it was all pre-arranged and whatever the problem, the same sow would take the initiative.

Our particular sow and her young made a particularly appealing picture as they went after the main group; the youngsters, all black, all in single file, might have been playing follow the leader. But this was no game. This was real life. Survival.

Meantime, the boar, the only adult male of any real size, had also moved further away from me. He paused often to look about him or, rather, to sense or smell what was happening. Only when the last of the 40-odd pigs had vanished into the grass did he go after them—a rear guard then. And just like any good soldier on a mission behind enemy lines, he paused to check for any sign of pursuit before he too was gone from sight. I moved quickly after them and saw the grass moving as he made his way through it; I heard the other pigs conversing, and I saw the boar—once and briefly—as he crossed a patch of open ground. All wonderful stuff on Cape York Peninsula in the dry season of 1993.

Python Waterhole, Almost dusk

In the fast-failing light, when even the brightest colours of the water lilies are robbed of their true colours, the black boar had emerged from the scattered gum trees to drink at one of the many billabongs, lagoons, and other such watering places spread around the park. They have colourful names: Crocodile Waterhole, Barramundi Waterhole, Black Gun Waterhole, Mosquito Waterhole, Red Lily Lagoon and, among many others, Brolga Dam. The names of course go back to the station days.

Everywhere I went in Lakefield National Park there was an abundance of water, so growth was lush and prolific and the pigs I saw there—well in excess of 200—were almost always in top condition. Indeed, there was so much water in the park that it didn't really seem like the dry season at all. Why was that? In conversation with the ranger in charge, Ray Teece, it all came down to an abundance of rain. Between the previous December (1992) and the March of this year they had had about twice the usual rainfall. So the lagoons were filled to capacity by a record-breaking 160 centimetres of rain in a matter of a few months. Why, Ray said, there were some lagoons carrying water this year for the first time that he could recall.

Meanwhile, the black boar had moved to the water's edge, where he dipped the tip of his saucer-shaped snout into it and created a small but spreading ripple. He drank not in peasant-like gulps as a common workman might down a glass of ale but in a more refined and dignified manner, as befitting a country gentleman. He also appeared a little apprehensive. Fair enough. It would be difficult to find such a watering place in the park where the possibility that it was inhabited by a crocodile did not arise. Here in Python Waterhole, for instance, there were definitely crocodiles, one of them considered large, about 4.5 metres. A crocodile that length will weigh about 350 kg and its jaws when open are wide enough apart to completely engulf the head of the biggest wild boar and powerful enough

when they snap shut like a massive steel press to crush its skull.

But as I watched the boar turn away from the waterhole, I realised that wild pork—raw, of course—was not about to be featured on the menu tonight at Python Waterhole Café.

As the boar wandered off I lowered my Nikon 7x35 wide-angle fieldglasses and, tucking them inside my khaki shirt, wished it hadn't been so dark and that I could have photographed the boar drinking. Like the sow I had photographed earlier today, this pig, now a clear-cut silhouette as it topped a rise, was rangy, high-backed, with a very long snout; indeed, they may have been brother and sister.

Red Lily Billabong, The following evening

At the tail-end of what had been yet again a lovely, sundrenched day in Australia's tropical north, I moved slowly through a stand of paperbark trees. Presently, I observed a particularly large wallow and stopped to look at it more closely.

There were more or less two distinct pools of muddy water located close to Red Lily Billabong, a scenic gem not that far from Bizant Outstation. All around the wallow, and all along the edge of the billabong for that matter, the ground was chopped up by the passage of numerous pigs.

At the wallow some of the tracks indicated pigs had been here during the past 24 hours. Nearby, I noticed mud adhered like glue sticking to the rough-barked trunk of a small tree. I noticed with interest that the highest level of the dried mud was about a metre—or just more than that—above ground level. So it was consistent with the shoulder height of a large boar. It had been used last of all by a black boar; there were a few crinkly black hairs lodged in the mud.

As we have already read it is essential that pigs cool off in the heat and the act of wallowing will certainly bring untold relief to overheated bodies. Pigs, however, range far beyond the tropics. Up in the Snowy Mountains, for instance, they also wallow, and not just when it's hot, either. There are obviously other reasons then why pigs wallow.

Wallowing in fact is a part of any wild pig's lifestyle, a year-round ritual, perhaps a daily occurrence. To a pig an extended wallow is obviously a most pleasurable experience, like you or I enjoying a long soak in a hot tub. Among other animals of the same inclinations are the rhinoceros, elephant, domestic pig (if given the opportunity), and in the Top End, water buffalo.

For us, and for them, a lengthy soak eases out any aches (ageing animals are just as prone to stiffening joints as we are but, unfortunately, can take no internal remedies to moderate the pain); so it makes us feel good, more relaxed, better able to cope with life in general. Fundamentally there isn't a great deal of difference between man and beast.

In hot climates—Lakefield National Park, for instance—there are all sorts of blood-sucking and biting insects and assorted parasites such as ticks that cause pigs untold stress. So not only does a wallow cool an overheated body, bringing relief and a sensation of well-being, but a layer of dried-off mud helps the pig to rid itself of troublesome pests by rubbing against the serrated bark of a tree. This largely circular rubbing motion, carried out energetically, also serves to harden the skin after the inevitable softening-up caused by a prolonged mud bath. Pigs tend to use the same rubbing trees year in, year out, and so given sufficient time they not only remove the bark from the tree but also the inner wood, resulting in deep, shoulder-shaped indentations. Due to excessive rubbing a tree may eventually snap in half.

By looking closely at such rubbing trees, you may spot the knife-like marks caused by a boar's tusks. He does not rub his tusks here and in this fashion to sharpen them but merely to warn off other boars. Right, it's all to do with territory. However, I was unable to find any such marks on the back-rubbing tree at the pig wallow close to Red Lily Billabong as the sun slipped out of sight beyond a tree-fringed skyline to the west. I was perhaps in a pensive frame of mind as I turned away from the wallow and started along a game trail—with the wind in my face—which followed the edge of the lily-fringed billabong. The reason for my mood of brief melancholy was that—in the morning—my extended trip to Lakefield National Park would be over and with Graham Hardwicke I would be returning to Cairns. However, I would be calling in at Cooktown, where Captain James Cook almost certainly did not liberate pigs in 1770, and, beyond there, Cape Tribulation, where there was a very good chance pigs were in residence

before the *Endeavour* ran into strife on the Great Barrier Reef.

But my sadness at the idea of leaving such a wonderful place was but a fleeting thing—I mean, how could I remain deflated when I took everything into consideration?

The water lilies, I noted, were especially lovely in full or even partial bloom. The same thing could not be said of the damage caused by pigs which here—as in many parts of the park—was excessive.

According to National Parks staff, pigs in Lakefield National Park are guilty of the following:

Pigs root up and consume plants, particularly those plants with extensive roots/tubers found in swamps and lagoons. Pigs consume water lilies, particularly those with tubers or bulbs and other aquatic vegetation. Entire swamps miles long have been completely ploughed up. Ploughing up of mud also prevents the growth of grasses at the edge of swamps, as the water level drops during the wet season . . . The main damage is through habitat destruction and severe competition for food—for example, with brolgas and magpie geese.'

Interestingly enough, that report dates from the late 1970s/early 1980s and is as relevant today as it was then.

The light was fading fast now—too fast, but all too typical of tropical regions whatever the season. Hmmm . . . unless I soon turned about and made fast tracks in the direction of camp I'd still be on the fringes of the billabong after dark. Dark? Close to a billabong in prime crocodile country? Forget it, sport!

Pausing in mid-stride, I checked my wristwatch—right, in ten minutes—no longer—I would turn about. So I went on with my telephoto camera contained in a foam-lined case within the small canvas daypack I invariably carry with me on field trips such as this.

I had covered perhaps 200 metres when—upwind—there was a squeal. Pigtalk! Quickly but with care I pussyfooted to where my field of view suddenly extended and there I saw a saddle-backed sow and her mud-dripping young breaking away from a small wallow formed within the perimeter of the billabong itself.

With a chuckle, I watched the last of the piglets vanish into heavy cover, could hear the sow conversing in scolding tones. What a particularly nice way to end the day, I thought.

12 In Arnhem Land

It is possible that an increase in the pig population will follow a reduction in buffalo. The ability of pigs to multiply rapidly must be considered in implementing a buffalo control programme.

Kakadu Plan of Management, Australian National
Parks and Wildlife Service, 1980

'Pigs!' Michael Clarke hissed excitedly as the Toyota pitched and swayed across a huge, sunbaked, pig-devastated flood plain somewhere between the East Alligator River and Coopers Creek in Arnhem Land.

Wrestling vigorously with the steering wheel, Max Davidson glanced sideways past me at his dark-haired son-in-law and rasped, 'Where?'

By way of an answer, Michael pointed dead ahead through the grimy, insect-splattered windscreen towards a sun-hazed, mirage-like tree line, and Max, narrowing his already squinting eyes, the better to see, muttered, 'Buggered if I can see them!'

'They're there, all right,' Michael shot back with confidence.

'Phil?' Max nudged me with his elbow.

I simply shook my head in the negative and Max grunted deep in his considerable chest.

On went the gutsy Toyota, slamming into one deep, pig-created hole after another, jolting out of it, so that what should have been a pleasant drive through a stunning wilderness area in the region of Mt Borradaile was more of an endurance test.

Presently, the tree line was close enough to take real form and Michael's rather handsome face now wore an expression of doubt.

'Where's your pigs now?' Max asked almost triumphantly.

'They've turned to stone,' Michael admitted sheepishly, meaning the slim, 26-year-old hunting guide had mistaken several low rocks scattered about for the hump-like shapes of foraging pigs.

'Now wouldn't that rock ya,' Max said, straight-faced. Even Michael laughed at that one.

With a final, spine-wrenching jolt the four-wheel-drive came to a halt. Max switched off the ignition.

'About time, too,' I said, pulling a wry face.

'Rough as guts, all right,' Max said, grinning through his Father Christmas-like beard. Max looks a whole lot like the late Ernest Hemingway. A learned type, called 'the professor' up here; not, I would learn, without very good reason.

A lean type of about average height and early middle age climbed down nimbly enough from the open, safari-style back of the vehicle. Hans Fuchs fingered his moustache thoughtfully, re-slung his rifle, and looked at Max with raised eyebrows.

Max hitched up his somewhat floppy shorts with a great air of purpose and said to his Swiss client:

'Let's go find you a wild boar, eh?' While there were few words of English Hans understood, 'wild boar' didn't pose any such problems and his dark eyes flashed with all the anticipation of a child about to open an expensive-looking birthday present.

Max looked at me. 'Okay?'

'As I'll ever be, Max.'

He glanced at my camera bag. 'Enough film with you?'

'You worry about finding Hans a boar and let me concern myself with the photography, huh?'

With a smile, Max spun on his heel. He started off in loping strides, as befitting a real bushman. He followed the edge of an escarpment, the sun low down on his right, casting a fiery glow on the mesa-like rock formations, all reds and golds, gleaming as though burnished across the mostly dried-up floodplains where the growth resembled Mitchell grass in southwest Queensland, shining on a large stretch of swampy country fringing the trees. The wetlands were alive with birds, hundreds and hundreds of birds, perhaps thousands of them. And the further we went, the more we heard their clamourous sounds.

Out here, beyond the East Alligator River, Max and Philippa Davidson run a first-rate tourist operation, which caters for a wide range of interests. In their own words:

> A Mt Borradaile Arnhemland Adventure is no predictable package, but an exclusive experience moulded to suit your particular interest, be it exploring, rock art, Aboriginal bush tucker and culture, wildlife, photography, barramundi fishing, bird watching or just soaking up the atmosphere of this unique wilderness lifestyle.
>
> Mt Borradaile is so unique, with an environment that must be protected for posterity, that the Aboriginal custodians will allow only 15 visitors per day to enter the area.

Among the 'wildlife' mentioned in the above publicity blurb are of course wild pigs. Many wild pigs. Perhaps more wild pigs between the East Alligator River and Coopers Creek than there have ever been. All reason enough for the likes of professional hunting guide Max Davidson, in line with both the thinking and policy of the traditional land owners, to encourage overseas hunters like Hans Fuchs to visit here.

Now, Max and Hans, side by side, their shadows elongated by the ever-sinking sun, were a little ahead of Michael and I. As they swung wide to skirt a big outcrop of rock, I saw Max pause and stand stock still. By the sudden tense set of his shoulders, I knew he had seen something. He was raising to his eyes a pair of miniature Leupold fieldglasses when we linked up with them.

'Max?' Michael said.

'Boar.'

'Good one?'

'Promising.'

Meantime, I was shading my eyes from the sun, staring hard in the direction Max was glassing. There! A small but telltale black hump in the green of the swamp. And beyond there, I saw two more dark shapes.

'Couple more further on,' Max said. 'They could be boars, too.Looking good, all right.' He lowered the 9x25s and turned to Hans, who was so eager to move he resembled a straining guard dog held on a too-tight leash. Max, grinning, held up a thumb in the universal gesture: everything in the garden was A-okay. A hard predatory smile crossed Hans' face.

Who said the Swiss weren't warlike?

'Damnitall!' Max had suddenly lost his winning smile. No carefully thought-out stalk on an unsuspecting animal was about to take place here. Indeed no! For the boar was already on the move. Wind? No, I doubted that he had smelled us. Perhaps there was another reason for his abrupt departure. His sixth sense, perhaps. Whatever the reason it didn't really matter, did it?

I tapped Hans on the arm. 'What're you like with that'—I indicated his rifle—'at 800 yards?' Hans looked blankly at me.

Max flashed me a mock baleful look: bush humourists he didn't really need.

One thing working in our favour was that the boar wasn't running flat out; rather, he was forging through the muddy ground at a fast and totally deceptive clip.

The question was: could we—that is, Hans—more or less head the boar off and get within good shooting range before it reached the comparative sanctuary of the escarpment.

Well, there was but one way to find out and Max snapped 'C'mon!' and, beckoning Hans to follow him, set off at a hard run.

By now it was clear exactly where the boar was running to: an extension of the wetlands that probed like a pointing finger into the rocky ground. In effect, the escarpment resembled the crumbling fortifications of an ancient European castle that Hans' distant ancestors might have fought over with far more primitive weapons than the .338 calibre Winchester Model-70 rifle he was carrying this evening.

So much of my attention was centred on the boar that I was hardly aware of Michael's elbows pumping by my side as we ran neck to neck in that energy-sapping humidity. I felt a hand brush my arm.

'Over there!'

'Huh?'

'Look—over—there!'

Breaking speed, I swivelled my head and by following the line of his pointing finger I saw what he was indicating: a pig climbing up out of the far swamplands, up into the ember-like red rocks, a black boar with unusually long legs. He moved freely and with agility, like an accomplished mountaineer. He vanished amidst a jumble of rocks, a ghost pig, perhaps, like something unreal, an apparition conjured up by a too-imaginative mind. You see, I was convinced there and then that this was by far the biggest wild boar I had ever seen and later when I expressed these thoughts to Michael he said that he'd never seen a boar to match that one.

For reasons unknown, the boar we were following actually slowed down as it entered the inlet-shaped extension of the wetlands. A gaggle of magpie geese—like a black and white cloud—lifted into the sky with insane cackles. By now, Hans and Max, shoulder to shoulder, had reached a massive rock more or less hemming in one side of the inlet. By peering around it, they saw the boar directly across from them. It had angled across the boggy ground to a well-used game trail linking the floodplains to the inner sanctuary of the escarpment. The trail ran under a rim-like rock wall.

With haste, Hans flopped himself over a roundish rock, the better to steady himself.

The boar was running but only slowly, one or two kilometres an hour above a fast gait.

'Shoot!' Max said between gritted teeth.

Hans fired.

A 210-grain projectile struck the rockface like a guided missile, breaking off scaly bits of rock, about half a metre above the boar's head. Much too high then to give it a permanent headache.

Again Hans fired, this time as the boar moved even more slowly because of the way the trail narrowed and was partly blocked by a rockfall.

Another clean miss.

Max turned pale under his ruddy tan: he was going through every hunting guide's worst nightmare.

At the far end of the inlet the soft ground gave way to a dry sandy channel winding off into the rocks and here the boar, as though checking out its backtrail, spun about. It stood in a challenging attitude, chest heaving, long, straight tail swishing from side to side in the manner of an aggressive lioness. You had to admire him.

So the boar was a standing target at less, I judged, than 200 metres.

This time, Hans, m'boy.

So for a third time Hans, having shifted his position so that he had an even better support from which to shoot, triggered off a third shot.

This particular shot sounded much louder, the racket filling the inlet, slamming back and forth off the rock walls closing it in.

Almost instantly the boar had whirled about, a jackknifing motion that saw him hesitate for a milli-second and then barrel into thick undergrowth.

Max lifted his heavy shoulders in a resigned

fashion and the expression that flooded his face might have been that of a drowning man going down for the third time. Whatever was going on in his mind, however, stayed right there.

Meantime, Hans looked perplexed as he studied his rifle. How on earth could he have missed three shots? He looked at Max in an apologetic fashion.

I patted Hans on the shoulder in a sympathetic manner.

'Maybe you were breathing too hard, eh?' But Hans of course couldn't understand what I'd said.

'Better make sure you missed,' Max sighed heavily. Right, you always have to make sure of that.

But as we all knew deep down—a trusty gut reaction—that particular boar was unharmed. Luck of the draw, right? On another day, and given the same set of circumstances, a skilled rifleman would have taken him out with one shot, no worries. But all due credit to this boar, for he'd run the .338 gauntlet and lived to tell about it.

Checking for signs to the contrary had taken us well up the dry sandy-bottomed channel—a raging creek when the big rains came. Pigsign was heavy here, their tracks leading to, and coming from, the floodplain. Indeed, you could actually smell pigs on the wind's pent-up breath, the smell of *Sus scrofa* and not your farmyard variety. The smell, I noted, was especially powerful around, and in the vicinity of, a wallow: a solidly formed wallow, like a communal bathhouse of Roman times. I suspected that generations of pigs had put it to good use.

With a sweeping gesture, Max, as though playing a part in a theatrical production, said that around this particular area the pigs camped in caves and in hollows under rocks—a top spot to escape the heat of the day.

'Always a great spot for boars,' Max added, looking with interest at a particularly large heap of droppings.

'Like that, y'mean?'

'Yeah—exactly like that.' He looked at Hans, who nodded in a sensible manner but, as always, or almost always, remained silent. Nor did Hans appear to smile very much. Well, there hadn't been a reason for braying laughter yet, had there?

'I suppose all this is under water in the wet?' I asked.

'Just about.'

''So where do pigs go?'

'The high ground, of course.'

Above: The Asian origins of this sow in Lakefield National Park are only too evident.

Above right: A wild boar ridding itself of dried mud by rubbing against the bark of a rubbing tree.

Right: A wild boar digging industriously for roots/ bulbs at the edge of the billabong shown above.

Twin pig wallows close to a lily-fringed billabong in Lakefield National Park.

Red water lily in flower.

Billabong in the region of Mt Borradaile.

Michael Clarke near where he and the author saw perhaps the biggest wild boar they had ever seen.

The author's Arnhem Land boar.

Time stood still in this place of ancient Aboriginal rockpaintings.

At Mt Borradaile safari camp.

Max (*front*) and Hans make double-quick time across a floodplain burnished with late evening sun.

A triumphant Hans.

High ground? It was my turn to look perplexed. 'There isn't too much of that around here, is there?' I mean, even the topmost level of the escarpment wasn't that much higher than the floodplain.

'True,' Max admitted, with the hint of smile, 'there isn't. You could say that what high ground there is tends to get rather overcrowded in the wet.'

'I bet the pigs're pretty skinny by the time it's over.'

'They could use a good feed, all right.'

Presently, we were making our way back towards the floodplain, following the same trail the fortunate boar had taken. Along here Max instructed Michael to return to the vehicle, to take it to the far side of the floodplain, where we had entered it and of course closer to camp, and to wait for us there.

'Might be dark by the time we get there,' Max finished up saying.

'Don't worry,' Michael said, turning on his heel, 'I won't go home without you.'

With a good-natured grin, Max shook his fist at Michael's retreating back. 'Cheeky young bastard,' he muttered.

'Weren't we all,' I said, sounding like Socrates on one of his less inspired days.

And with the westering sun almost hidden beyond a rocky skyline, and Michael well on his way, we trooped along a linking game trail. The trail more or less skirted the floodplain, passing through thick scrub, zigzagging through outcrops of rock where tall trees shed their bark.

Again, there was a great deal of pigsign, the dusty trail crisscrossed with the passage of countless animals. I signalled to Max.

'Pig highway.'

'Huh?' Like many hunters, Max is a trifle deaf—too much high-calibre muzzleblast in his eardrums, I expect.

'Plenty of pigs,' I near shouted. 'Y'know, Route 66 and all that.'

'Oh, yeah, plenty of pigs, all right.'

It was possible that the level of conversation would improve, if only marginally, with a few beers in camp later on.

The sight of two black pigs foraging in the swamps was a reason for sudden excitement in the ranks. Max quickly confirmed they were both boars. Boars. Hans' eyes were aglow with expectancy again.

I realised, then, that a short distance beyond the further one was the rocky outcrop where Michael and

I had seen that huge boar perhaps an hour ago. Where was he now? I wondered.

'Wind's right.' Max's pleased voice barely lifted above a whisper.

Hans nodded as though he understood. Perhaps he had taken a crash course in English since missing those three shots?

Max appeared to consider and I had an idea (which he later confirmed was right) that given the extremely flat-shooting capabilities of the .338 Magnum cartridge, under almost any other circumstances you care to name, he would not have hesitated to instruct his client to take a shot from here. But Hans of course was no ordinary client. His confidence was possibly at an all-time low after what had happened, shot to pieces.

At that point the furthest boar started to lose interest in feeding. He looked about him and then turned away and started towards a belt of timber. There were no signs of alarm on his part and we were thankful for that. The other boar hadn't even lifted his head, just went on grubbing industriously, digging up roots, bulbs, whatever.

In simple English, but with excessive hand movements, Max explained to Hans that they would make a detour and attempt to come in on the boar from an entirely different angle—that is, to end up at the tree line we were looking directly across the swamps at, close to where one of the boars had just vanished. From there, I knew, it would be a rather simple shot in comparison with one from this particular spot. Again Hans gave every impression he knew what Max had said.

We moved quickly but with stealth too along the continuing gametrail which after a short distance began to form a loop. In places the trail was overgrown with flowering regeneration and the mere act of brushing aside branches could, and did, have nasty results. So down came a veritable shower of green tree ants, flaking one's shoulders like an unusually coloured dandruff. Worse, they somehow scurried inside the open collar of your shirt and instead of stinging like the also-present mosquitoes bit hard enough to make you wince. That's hunting in the tropics for you.

Finally, we started to swing back towards the swamplands. Perhaps as much as ten to fifteen minutes had gone by since we had last seen the boar. Ten minutes? He could be long gone by now, perhaps, had he ran fast enough, to have caught up with the boar Hans had missed and exchanged words over the day's events. Three shots, eh? My, weren't you a lucky fellow!

Carefully, we sneaked through the last of the trees, the swamplands opening up, dark near the start of the lush growth the pigs fed on but ablaze with the last of the sun perhaps 50 metres out.

And the boar was there!

I sensed rather than saw Hans' sudden tension.

Max indicated from where Hans should shoot, and, nodding, Hans crept forward until he was kneeling next to a paperbark tree, using that to rest the stock of the rifle against.

Now as I turned my attention to the boar the very last of the sun was casting a net over most of the swamplands, a golden haze, a little unreal. And even the boar, his coat burnished, glowing, might have had a fairy-tale wand cast over him, creating a magical spell.

I turned to Hans and saw his trigger finger tighten and suddenly hard reality replaced illusion and the boar was down where it stood, kicking in the mud, frantic actions until there was a final stillness.

With the sound of the shot still ringing in my ears, Hans had reloaded and dashed out into the open, ready to shoot again if need be. He unloaded the .338 as a beaming Max walked out of the trees and extended a hand to offer his congratulations; Hans took it and even managed to work up a big smile all of his own.

I looked back to the swamps, past the dead boar that would never again experience a sunrise. The sky, a particularly lovely sunset, was alive with birds, mostly in V-shaped formations, going home to roost.

Tonight, long after we had gone, scores and scores of pigs would emerge from the escarpment country to feed in the ever-shrinking swamplands. Dingoes would be about, too. In the billabongs saltwater crocodiles would be active. Yes, all out there on Max and Philippa Davidson's hunting concession located between the East Alligator River and Coopers Creek in the Mt Borradaile region of Arnhemland.

The golden-coloured dingo made a particularly arresting sight as it paused in mid-stride near a lily-clad lagoon in the watershed of the East Alligator River. It was evening and starting to cool off after a very hot day. A fine time to be out hunting and, to judge by the amount of fresh pig rooting fringing the lagoon, pigs weren't that far away.

On each of the four nights I spent at Max and Philippa Davidson's comfortable, well-appointed safari camp near Mt Borradaile itself, I was awoken by dingoes.

In regard to the feral pig/dingo relationship the previously mentioned Dr Max King had some interesting comments to make.

'Pig populations up here are essentially controlled by dingoes,' King says. 'They follow the pigs all the time—knocking off piglets—and that's the main reason why they don't explode in numbers.

'In some areas where there's less pressure from dingoes their numbers can be simply enormous—mobs of a hundred are far from uncommon today and only recently I heard of 1500 pigs being more or less grouped together.'

Fifteen hundred feral pigs?

'Yes, I know that's hard to imagine,' he continued with a smile, 'but the report is reliable enough.' He then explained that the incredible number of pigs had been observed in the Moyle River country, near Port Keats. 'Course it's all Aboriginal land out there,' he added. Then: 'A mate of mine, Jim Metcalf, got back yesterday from a trip down the Daly River. They saw several mobs of 50 animals and and in one group Jim reckons there was at least 200.' He shook his head. 'Big mobs up here at the present time,' he finished, slipping easily into Top End jargon to describe large numbers of practically anything.

Dr Max King—articulate, friendly, and darn good company—believes like many that the extremely large numbers of feral pigs at present in the Top End—perhaps an all-time high in many areas—can be directly attributed to the sad demise of the water buffalo inasmuch as there is now virtually no competition between the species for habitat or food. Also, the present high population of dingoes, King says, can be put down to the large numbers of pigs. One big merry go round then, isn't it?

(The only other predator of the feral pig in Australia's tropical north not so far mentioned is the python (*Python amethyitinus*) which is known to prey on piglets and dingo pups.)

In the draining, stifling heat of midafternoon (and it was still officially winter!), Max Davidson, with enormous pride and untold respect, took me to a well hidden place that until quite recently was unknown to European man. Here was a maze of rocks, weatherbeaten, misshapen. Within the rocks were many caverns, and in some of them the brittle bones of long dead Aborigines were placed in a ceremonial fashion on narrow ledges above the dust-choked earth. Time stood still here, ceased to exist, and in this most sacrosanct place you moved quietly and spoke in quiet tones and were very careful not to touch anything you shouldn't for fear that the unseen guardians would eventually take their terrible revenge.

'Watch your head,' Max whispered as we stooped under a ledge and into a large cave—a main burial ground; a skull, lying half-buried in the dust, appeared to be grinning up at me: I did not feel inclined to return the smile.

There were magnificent examples of Aboriginal rock art to be seen and marvelled at here, and some of the vivid paintings on the cliffs and under rocky overhangs were in such awkward places that you wondered why the artist had chosen such a spot to demonstrate his art and, secondly, how on earth he or she had actually managed to paint it so well there.

Among the paintings Max showed to me at some length were a number that related to comparatively recent times, the arrival of the white man, for instance. One painting in particular was of a pair of single-shot Martini Henry rifles dating to the early buffalo hunting era. Such a weapon in .303 calibre was used by Paddy Cahill in the days before he crossed the East Alligator River at what later became known as Cahills Crossing and took up residence at a not too distant Oenpelli.

Despite the fact that wild pigs had been in the watershed of the East Alligator River from around—and possibly well before—the turn of the century, there were no paintings here that included pigs. Nor for that matter is there an Aboriginal word for pig.

A Professor J. Colson, who studied Aboriginal rock shelters and middens here in Arnhem Land and on Cape York Peninsula, wrote these relevant words in 1981:

> The faunal records of the final prehistoric period in northern Australia are not admittedly as extensive as one might wish, and they are better for Arnhem Land than for Cape York. I have just finished the editing of a manuscript for publication which describes the excavation of a rockshelter near Laura. This is the best and best-studied faunal suite for tropical Queensland (even though the fauna is pretty sparse). There is no pig here and none in the Arnhem Land sites.

The steamy heat was still very much evident when we tramped away from the place of the dead and primitive artwork that might last indefinitely and returned to the real living, breathing world.

Matching strides, for we are about the same height, Max and I came to the fringes of a big billabong. It was almost always a top spot to see pigs in the evening, Max said. I nodded at that, feeling very much the big white hunter (or at least an average-sized one) as I nursed the same .338 rifle Hans (now departed with his small set of tusks) had used. The thing was, Max was dead keen for me to account for an Arnhem Land boar and I saw nothing wrong with that line of thinking at all.

Naturally, we'd been unsure about the rifle Hans had used: was it, or was it not, sighted in accurately enough. One way to find out. Lacking a benchrest, I'd simply stood upright and supported the stock against the side of a tree and, aiming at a minor blemish you could easily cover with your hand on the trunk of a similar gum tree about 70 paces away, I'd fired. I'd been rather surprised by the lack of recoil considering the .338 is such a powerful calibre, and well satisfied to see that I'd hit my mark, not that there was anything left of it, you understand.

At any rate, it was much too early to see wild game up and about. They generally became active about late afternoon, Max reckoned. Even so, there was of course every possibility we might stumble across a boar in any one of a number of places it could have chosen to rest up in: a gloomy cave, amidst a big clump of tussock-like grass, or simply having a whale of time in a wallow.

'Let's go,' Max said with a smile.

And basically we did stumble across a boar, or, to be more accurate, a boar and sow. This is how it happened. We were trudging through sand, a thick coating that formed the base of a dry sandy wash—like a well defined road—that passed through jumbled up boulders the size of small cottages in an old English village where swineherds might once have called out: 'Here Pig! Pig! Pig!'

The two pigs, meantime, were resting up in a roomy cave, the mouth of which overlooked the route we were taking and was about one metre higher than the sandy bottom. By the sign I later checked out, the pigs were lying snout to snout and facing the way we were approaching from. As we drew level with the cave, two options were open to the pigs: they could've kept quiet and shrunk back from sight and, had that been the case, we would never have seen them or, and this is what they did, they could make a break for it.

So there we were, Max and I, when to my left and in my peripheral vision a big black boar and a medium-sized black sow exploded from the mouth of the cave.

Instantly, I was twisting about to face them, the rifle leaping to my shoulder as though it had a mind of its own. But by then they were in low but thick scrub, a narrow band running down one side of the wash. They broke free of the scrub about 50 metres away, kicking up sand, and only the best snap-shot in the world might have been good enough to nail the boar before he vanished. As it was, the .338 remained silent.

Max grinned. 'Didn't waste much time, did they?'

'Couple of rockets,' I agreed, moving to the cave for a look-see. It was a nice little spot they had been resting in, dry, and, as expected, free of droppings.

I dropped back to join Max in the wash and he expanded a little on the habits of pigs up here and I nodded from time to time and presently we went on again, crunching through the sand, passing many similar caves where any number of pigs could have been hiding.

A little later, I left Max hunkered down in the shade and I went to investigate something of a headland probing out into a big lagoon that appeared perfect saltwater crocodile habitat.

As I sneaked along, feeling the old and once so familar juices starting to flow, I was thankful that I was so well armed. It is no exaggeration to say it is dangerous country up here. True, most wild game in the Top End will usually head in the other direction at the first inkling of man. But the boar that had taken on the two Queenslanders in Lakefield National Park recently and come off second best was still very much on my mind, and so, for that matter, were the details of yet another unprovoked wild pig attack I had unearthed from the files of the *Northern Territory News* even more recently, dated 11 November 1988.

Wild pig attacks camper

A man had a close shave recently when he was attacked by one of the Territory's most feared animals—a wild boar.

Although details are sketchy, the man is believed to have escaped with only cuts and scratches.

The man was camping outside the Nitmiluk Katherine Gorge National Park entrance last Sunday when the beast attacked.

Conservation Commission parks and wildlife head Tom Dacey said the man had been sitting on a chair around a campsite when the large black pig bolted from scrub land.

Mr Dacey said the boar made a beeline for the man, knocking him from his seat.

He said the pig may have bitten the man.

A park ranger treated the minor injuries at the scene. The man was advised to attend hospital for antibiotics.

But Mr Dacey addded: 'The man sald he was OK and was eager to continue on his camping trip.'

Makes you think rather hard, doesn't it?

Again, this was buffalo territory. True, the once great herds that until only recently ranged this floodplain country were no more—shot out. However, they were not entirely eliminated. On several occasions over the last two days we had seen fresh buffalo droppings, a reason for high excitement in the ranks. The few buffalo that remained here, Max believed, were bulls. They were cunning, elusive animals that knew all about helicopter gunships and, as a result were now larely nocturnal. So they kept a very low profile during daylight hours and because their thick greyish-coloured hides were very often caked with mud—for they dearly like a wallow—in thick cover you could darn near stand on one before you were aware of it. So spook it then and it just might be ornery enough to leap up, and, horns swinging, bowl you over like skittled ninepins. In a situation like that the problem might be getting up again.

And naturally there were crocodiles about. Like the pigs, they too were perhaps at an all-time high, in their particular case the result of a long period of protection.

The thing is, not all saltwater crocodiles are found in the water, and while you'd be dead unlucky to come across one on dry land, with water so close that possibility could not be overlooked.

Wild boars!

Buffaloes!

Crocodiles!

I looked about me at great length and patted the gleaming walnut stock of the Winchester, deriving untold reassurance from the act.

Slowly, I came to the edge of the lagoon. It was fringed with water lilies. Birds of many species were out there. Wonderful!

I started along the paperbark tree-lined edge of the lagoon and within less than a minute spotted a sow just ahead of me—upwind, naturally. Several piglets appeared as I crouched down, the rifle across my drawn-up knees, my finger inside the trigger guard.

Boar?

Another sow appeared, grunting. She was off-white in colour, half grown, too young to conceive. There was a strong possibility she and the bigger, fully mature sow were related.

With surprise, I counted ten—no, eleven—piglets grouped around the sow, all very much the same size, same general colour. One litter? Why not? At the present time big litters were being reported all over the Top End, due of course to ideal breeding conditions.

Putting down the rifle, and pretty sure that a boar wasn't with the group, I removed my daypack and from it took out my camera, attached to which was a 135 mm lens, ideal for close-range photography. Then on hands and knees, I moved up on the unsuspecting pigs. Eventually, I was so close to a piglet that I was almost close enough to it to reach out a hand and pat it on the head: Hey, little buddy!

Even here in what might seem a no-risk situation I was taking a chance: a sow is not only a very caring mother but she is also a highly protective one, given to untold aggression should the situation warrant it. One hint of fear from the young one I was so close to and its mother—less than five metres away and busily rooting—just might rush to its side—which, as far as I was concerned, might prove bad news indeed. Consider this 1993 Reuters world-wide press release if you will:

Pig bites man

An angry pig savaged a British jogger yesterday, leaving him in hospital with two broken ribs and a gaping thigh wound. The jogger had disturbed the sow and her piglets rooting for acorns in the undergrowth of the New Forest. 'The sow bowled him over and trampled him before biting him and taking a big lump of flesh out of his thigh,' a police spokesman said. 'It was quite a savage attack.'

Slowly the small group of pigs moved further away from me, the sow nudging one of her piglets with her nose—a gentle, caring gesture and I was reminded of a touching little story which appeared in the previously mentioned *Natural History of the Pig*.

When too small to follow her, a sow will convey her young to safety as a cat does—in the mouth. During a farm fire in a suburb of Chicago a sow attempted to rescue her family from a burning barn. She was seen emerging from the structure carrying in her mouth a little one but a few hours old, making three trips successfully; but after returning for the fourth piglet, she never came out again.

Picking up the .338, and wondering just what was the true ancestry of pigs in the watershed of the East Alligator River, I rejoined Max Davidson.

Next morning was again lovely and warm, a carbon copy of the previous day and most likely exactly what it would be like a week from today.

Still with a trophy boar uppermost in our minds, we returned to the same general area of the big floodplain where Hans Fuchs had taken a boar.

In rainforest conditions—all dark and gloomy— we startled a huge mob of pigs that had in all probability visited the nearby swamplands overnight. Pigs in fact seemed to be running in all directions, a whole line of boars crossing my line of vision—left to right—as though I were in a fairground shooting gallery and they were metallic cutouts moving on an invisible track.

'Take one!' Max implored.

Sure thing, Max, I thought, but which one? You see, there were at least eight or nine boars running in line and they all appeared about the same size—that is, somewhere between 80 and 90 kg on the hoof, and they were all compact of build and they were all black. Any one of them could have carried a trophy set of tusks because boars in this watershed were renowned for them and, again, boars this size tend to be the real trophy tuskers.

So this would be a standing shot, and, because of that, my confidence might have been on a par with that of Hans when he'd lined up for a fourth time.

I heard Max, standing just behind me, draw a breath as I swung the .338 from left to right on a parallel course to that of the running boars, now bolting through tangled vines and some low fern, and I touched the trigger and the rifle shoved back against my shoulder and its report was loud in that closed-in situation and the boar I'd chosen to shoot at lurched and then staggered and then fell in a heap because it was hit through both shoulders and already dead and Max was slapping me on the shoulder and grinning and that grin grew heaps bigger when we saw that the boar's dark-stained tusks were a particularly fine Arnhem Land trophy.

PART THREE
IN WILD PIG COUNTRY

13 Plains Country

Due West of Hay, Western New South Wales

The lignum swamp covered a goodly portion of Torry Plaines' 65 000 acres. Back in 1952 when the Hodgson family had taken on the poorly fenced property, lignum scrub had pretty much covered the entire station.

It hadn't been easy raising sheep in those days in this part of the country. Indeed, they eventually gave up lambing on the station as a bad job and, instead of losing 75 per cent of lambs to rampaging pigs with an insatiable craving for sweet fresh meat, they'd taken the pregnant ewes via a back route to a pig-free station near Swan Hill and six months after the lambs were born, when the youngsters were big, strong and healthy, mothers and offspring had been brought back home.

You don't have to tell Barry Hodgson, who owns the station today, just what wild pigs can get up to!

At any rate, the lignum swamp covered an extensive plain that was, and had been for many years, a refuge for grey kangaroos, foxes, emus and, of course, feral pigs. The pigs as much as anything else were to be expected, for the station in a direct line is no real distance from where the Lachlan River loses its identity in the much bigger Murrumbidgee. At the confluence of these two rivers can be found a stupendous swamp system. It is considered one of the more significant breeding grounds of *Sus scrofa*

in the entire state and in good times, when water is abundant and feed plentiful, the pig population can number in the many thousands.

The lignum swamp is the focal point of my visit to Torry Plaines . . .

In any event, I had arrived at the nerve-centre of Torry Plaines on a fine winter's afternoon, the crispness in marked contrast, and all the better for it, with the rising humidity I'd experienced so recently in the Top End.

There was movement at the station and the word had got around that about 5000 of the station's 20 000 merino sheep were about to be trucked off the place, and that, beyond Hay, they would be unloaded on the side of the road and would thereupon become the responsibility of drover Jim Tracey.

You could say that this scenario was being played out over much of the western part of the state: there was not enough feed to go around on the big stations, the result of a two-year drought, and consequently most of the stock, sheep and cattle, were being 'walked' around the well established stock routes—that is, the wide areas of open range fringing backcountry roads, an area of ground known as 'the long paddock'.

I had been told all this by Mick Williams, as he and his wife Debbie (Barry Hodgson's daughter), and a general hand, Gary Smith, were in the dusty yards working with some of the outward-bound sheep.

When I'd expressed surprise to Mick about the number of drovers I'd seen on the roads, so to speak, out this way, he'd said that the droving scene was as strong as ever in western New South Wales.

Presently they'd finished with the sheep and, glad of a real break, 40-year-old Mick, a city boy who'd been out west for over 20 years, said, yeah, there were still plenty of pigs on the station—enough, anyway, for hunters to be on the place every single weekend. To a man these hunters came from out of state—Melbourne mostly (400 kilometres away). Indeed, the Hay district—a flat, treeless, saltbush plain with a 360 degree skyline—has long been a mecca for Victorian-based hunters who tend to find their own populations of pigs much too scattered and inconsistent in numbers to rely on for what might be termed 'regular good sport'.

Jacking a thumb at Gary's departing back, Mick said:

'Listen, mate, he and Robert're goin' out after pigs later on, I think. Why don't you go out with them?' This offer was as unexpected as was my arrival at the station.

'Would they mind?'

Mick's eyebrows shot up. 'Mind! You've gotta be kidding?' He paused. 'It could be pretty late by the time you get back, but.'

Debbie, who had just joined us, was nursing baby William.

'Do you have to get back to town tonight?' she asked. I shook my head, no. 'Then why not stay here tonight?' she suggested. Then: 'Pity Dad's away; he'd have loved talking to you about pigs.'

'You'd have never stopped him,' Mick said with a laugh.

'Sounds great,' I said, 'and thanks.' I nodded at my rental car. 'I've got a swag with me.'

Mick laughed again. 'No worries then, is there?' he said.

Too true, there weren't any worries on Torry Plaines station one lovely late afternoon in July.

An hour or so later the woebegone red Daihatsu 4-wheel-drive ute, with three of us cramped in the coffin-like cabin and three dogs standing with eager anticipation on the far more roomy back, headed out with gears crunching and apparently minus any springs from the station headquarters towards the lowering sun, a fireball in the western sky.

Lodged behind the steeringwheel was 20-year-old Robert Nelson who was employed as a driver on the place, mostly heavy machinery. Born in Hay, Robert had been coming out here for many years before his mother and father found work on the station and landing a job here himself had been a real godsend for someone who liked to hunt pigs whenever he could.

'Ya know, we never miss out where we're going,' Robert said with the utmost confidence. 'Isn't that right, Gary?'

'Yeah.'

Gary, two years older than his mate, and much less talkative, hailed from nearby Balranald. He worked on the station on a mutually agreeable come and go basis. Mostly, however, he worked as a shearer.

'Me Dad was a shearer and me Mum was a shearers' cook,' he explained in one of his more chatty moments. 'I reckon shearing's in the blood, eh?'

Suddenly, I noticed a thick-coated red fox sitting on what appeared to be a partly submerged log and I drew it to the attention of my companions with a gesture. The fox, rather aloof looking, appeared to take not a scrap of notice of us passing by. Maybe it was thinking of the forthcoming lambing season on Torry Plaines and how tasty a newly born lamb was to eat. I rather expect a few pigs were tuned in to that same waveband, too.

'Cheeky bugger!' was Robert's rasping comment.

'Should've stopped and barrelled it,' Gary said matter of factly.

Stop the vehicle of course and that fox would be off like the proverbial shot.

Presently, we passed a big grain silo. At night, Robert said, pigs foraged around the base of the silo, feeding on the overspill. And if any full sacks of grain were left there then they would rip them open.

Now we jolted along a raised causeway. Ahead, a vast lignum swamp was coming into view. It appeared featureless and drab and extended in distance so that as we drew closer to it there was nothing but a wall of high, mostly interlocked scrub, bisected by channels of water, stretching to the horizon, perhaps 10 kilometres distant.

Robert removed his left hand from the steeringwheel and pointed at the swamp:

'That's the place I meant!' Robert exclaimed. He slapped the flat of his hand on the steering wheel for added emphasis and glanced sideways at his expressionless mate.

'Isn't that right, Gary?'

'Yeah.'

Off to our right were fields of crops—barley and wheat. Many grey kangaroos had been out feeding here on the still as yet short growth which, the way things were shaping up, wasn't going to reach anywhere near its full potential. The roos of course, with the sudden arrival of a vehicle, which they associated with deep trouble, were heading for cover: the sanctuary of the lignum swamp.

Gary's tanned face worked. 'Jeez—bloody roos!' he complained sourly.

Once again you don't have to tell Barry Hodgson or his son-in-law Mick Williams about roos. Roos? Hell's fire—they have to live with them on their doorstep and, if they weren't controlled, sharing a feed in the kitchen with you, too.

Mick Williams on the subject of too many roos:

'Course we have roo shooters here—professional blokes—but they're only allowed by law to take the big ones, and that means we've got to get out there and shoot them too.' He'd pulled a disgusted face then. 'It's not easy, you know. I mean, you work all day and then have to spend half the night shooting bloomin' roos to keep 'em off the crops.' After a lengthy pause, he'd added, 'If you don't do that—well—you'll go under.' Right, it was as simple as that out west.

Mick Williams could of course have been speaking for untold men on the land in New South Wales in the 1990s.

Presently, station staff on Torry Plaines were being issued with a permit to shoot 500 kangaroos each six weeks. At the time of my visit they were shooting 20–30 each night. The carcasses were left to rot where they were—dog tucker, Mick reckoned matter of factly, and added that the station dogs pretty much existed on roo meat these days. Roo meat? No wonder the three powerful-looking bruisers on the back of the ute looked so fit and healthy, I thought.

The track continued along the causeway—the roos rushing in panic from the crops, bounding past the bloated remains of their own kind, then, their powerful haunches propelling them up the loose earth of the embankment, leaping across the track before us, skittering down the far side, hopping through shallow water, clearing a sagging fenceline, and then vanishing into the protective wall of lignum scrub. Safe again, brother roo.

Following a sharp L-turn, we came to a halt. We clambered out. The dogs, to sharp, no-nonsense commands, sprang down from the back of the ute, to urinate in their ever-rising excitement against the wheels of the vehicle.

The canine hit team were a pretty typical trio of pigdogs that—above all else, the very bottom line—have both the inbred strength and gritty determination to hang on to a ferocious boar when push turns to shove and shove in turn becomes something far more serious. Overly intelligent these dogs weren't but courageous and brave and willing to put their lives on the line for their masters they most certainly were.

Spike, Gary's dog, was a bull mastiff/rottweiler cross; Bush was a rottweiler/bullterrier cross, and Pooch was a real mixture—mostly rottweiler but with a generous measure of other blood too, namely bullterrier, and, to a lesser degree, but of some significance in his makeup, greyhound and staghound.

'Pooch?' I said wonderingly to Robert.

'Yeah, Pooch.'

Well, Pooch he might have been as a silly young pup but 'Pooch' he most certainly wasn't as an adult animal.

In short, they were the kind of dogs, bred for aggression, that aren't too popular in the suburbs these days.

As we went down the embankment at a scramble, Gary said over his shoulder, 'You don't mind getting your feet wet, do you?' It seemed a rather inane question because a pool of water, too wide to skirt, lay between the embankment and the lignum.

'Course not!' I retorted, wondering just what he reckoned I was made of.

And so we, like the roos, crossed a shallow stretch of water and entered the strange world of the lignum scrub.

Already, I'd been aware of how much colder it was—chilly even—and I cursed myself for not bringing a sweater along. Still, I hadn't expected to go hunting today, and, another thing, only a week back I'd been in the Northern Territory and winter woollies up there tend to remain in your bag. No matter, I was wearing a cotton singlet and shirt and they would have to suffice. Besides, the way the boys were talking we'd nail a pig or two in double-quick time, the dogs barely raising a sweat.

For the most part the lignum—a rather spindly growth—stood about 2.5–3 metres high and grew in clumps; the ground between the clumps was soggy and when it wasn't that then there were those channels

Left: Max Davidson and the Arnhem Land country he loves so much.

Below: In the lignum swamps.

The township of Hay; the district has long been a mecca for pig hunters based in Victoria.

Above: On Torry Plaines station—Gary Smith (left) and Richard Nelson.

Right: Living the life of professional pig hunters are Geoff (*left*) and Brett Crowhurst; that's Yvette between them.

Below: Phillip Naughton at Merrimajeel station on the bank of the Lachlan River.

of water I've already mentioned to contend with. Wet feet? Crutch wet, more like!

Game trails were almost everywhere, a maze of them, confusion itself where we were concerned but linking routes for the likes of roos and pigs.

It was also quiet in the lignum. No wind. And no sun either now, the temperature taking a sudden drastic nosedive.

I came to a sudden halt: what was that noise, I asked? That, I was told, was the splashing sounds roos make as they crossed deep water. Because the view was so restricted, we couldn't see any roos, and yet we could hear them more and more now, the sounds coming from nearby and far away, all a little unnerving for a reason I didn't understand.

Again we had no other choice but to plunge into deep, icy-cold water, the dogs paddling frantically behind us, tongues lolling, loving every single moment of it.

'Shit—it's cold!' I moaned, afraid that I would slip and fall on the apparently clayey bottom of this 6 metre wide channel, a disaster because there was over $2000 worth of camera equipment around my neck.

The young pighunters, to whom all this special forces stuff was part and parcel of their chosen sport, laughed at my obvious discomfort.

Once they left the water, the dogs shook themselves with vigour, and then went on. Soon there was a growing, near tangible tension in their ranks. Pigs were about? Fresh tracks around a small wallow confirmed it; I noticed the equally-recent marks of a boar's tusks on the thin, sapling-sized trunk of a lignum bush. Leading away from the wallow was naturally enough a well used trail and the marks of the boar's passage resembled bootmarks in wet cement.

'Some pretty big boars out here,' Robert said, noticing my interest in the spoor.

Big boars?

Only last weekend a Victorian hunter who'd been coming out here for 15 years was having a high old time of it—with four pigs to his credit and now homeward bound—when his dogs came across a formidable boar. All might have worked out in a satisfactory manner if, the hunter thought, his dogs weren't already battle fatigued. But combat weary or not they were pigdogs after all and as such they were as game as bushrangers. In any event, one of the dogs—a spunky bull-terrier cross which the hunter

had had for six years and was a particular favourite— was ripped about so badly in the furious ruckus which developed that it had died in its master's arms as he had carried it out. The boar had lived to fight again.

All of a sudden, I realised that the dogs had gone, departed like columns of smoke on a windy day. Simultaneously, Robert flung up a hand in the warning manner of a buckskinned scout spotting a bunch of hostiles in Injun territory. He turned and his wide smile was pure satisfaction: told you so!

Quietness prevailed . . . a cathedral-like hush . . . then broken again by those rather unhinging sounds of unseen roos on the move. Just how many grey kangaroos were there out here? I couldn't help but wonder.

Five minutes went by.

Five more.

A thoughtful Robert fished inside his overalls and from a shirt pocket took out a crumpled packet of smokes. He lighted up with a thoughtful expression on his face: should've heard a bark by now? Gary crouched on his heels like a stockman at ease at a campfire. Campfire? My, I could've used a campfire right then.

Conditions were decidedly gloomy now, the sky heavily overcast. Rain? Why not? There had been plenty of the wet stuff—too much, really—now that the long drought was something for bushmen to reflect on over a beer instead of being a constant source of concern.

Robert's face, pinched with the nasty cold, worked as he stamped out yet another cigarette.

'Pretty bloody strange we haven't heard anything yet . . . ' He shook his head. 'Never been gone as long as this before.'

'Picked a helluva time to do it,' I said flatly, my water-logged R.M. Williams jeans sticking uncomfortably to my legs, plastered to my frozen butt. I shot a glance at my wristwatch: we had been in this spot for at least an hour, the boys alternatively shouting and whistling for their dogs to come back.

Anything, of course, could have happened to the dogs out there, the most likely scenario was that they had chased a big boar and were unable to stop him. But had that been the case, then we would surely have heard a bark? I mean, we were hearing roos— splash! splash! splash!—from several hundred metres away, and, given the conditions, perhaps much further away than that. They could also have run into the boar that just a few days ago had given a game little bull-terrier cross heaps. And maybe, my mind raced with possibilites, they were lost, scattered hell west and crooked (and Tom Cole didn't coin that particular phrase) in what to a baffled dog, his homing instincts shot to pieces, would have soon resembled a maze with no real way out of the confusion. And then—

'Wouldn't it piss you off!' Gary shook his head with disgust.

Not wrong, Gary, I thought.

'Maybe they're back at the ute,' Robert said brightly.

'Be bloody good if they were,' Gary said.

So in total darkness we blundered out of the lignum and it is true that I had no real idea where I was, no sense of direction, completely bewildered, relying on the locals to get me out of this cursed place.

Back on the causeway, the boys again cried out and whistled but the only reply was the noise of the roos and a plague of click-clacking crickets.

Pacing back and forth with agitated body movements which I sensed rather than saw, Robert said, 'How long've they been gone, mate?'

'At least an hour and a half,' Gary replied. 'Better take off for home, eh?'

'Suppose so,' Robert said with reluctance. He removed his overalls and placed them on the ground, the idea being that the dogs, should one or more return to where we had started out (which dogs usually do in such a situation), would recognise Robert's clothing by its smell and, all going to plan, would settle down there and wait to be picked up. 'Come back in the morning,' Robert added with a heavy sigh.

And so we returned to the station headquarters, arriving there about eight o'clock. I was numb with cold and, not having eaten since breakfast, hungry enough to tear into one of those roo carcasses out in the crop fields. But a hot shower, dry clothing (wrapped up in my swag in case of emergency) and a good feed soon put everything in perspective.

Later, I lay in my swag and reflected on the hunt. Something different, all right. I wondered what the dogs were doing, and I had a darn good idea those thoughts were not mine alone.

It was early next morning when I drove away from the station and so for all I know Spike, Bush and Pooch are still out there in that huge lignum swamp on Torry Plaines where untold numbers of grey kangaroos make oddly unsettling sounds as— unseen—they ford narrow channels of water . . .

Merrimajeel station, Booligal, 80 kilometres north of Hay

On the northern banks of a very discoloured Lachlan River, Phillip Naughton, whose family has long associations with the area made famous in one of Banjo Patterson's poems, explained that his property of 21 000 acres was once the western portion of Booligal station (established in 1911) before the giant-sized run was subdivided.

Specifically, Phillip's land, with the Lachlan River forming its southern boundary, was located in lower western New South Wales, while across the river was classed as the Riverina. There are no clear-cut records to say just when pigs established themselves in the wild in the Riverina but in all probability it had taken place by the late 1880s and certainly they were around Booligal before the turn of the century.

On Merrimajeel, which Phillip believes refers to one of two creeks north of the Lachlan and means a lignum/swampy creek, are run about 20 000 merino sheep, around one animal to the acre. There are some cross-bred cattle here, too. The property is typical of those fronting the Lachlan inasmuch as there is a pig problem here.

At times, Phillip says, mobs of pigs 40 strong are not uncommon but, as they tend to pass through the station rather than remaining for any length of time, they are difficult to pin down. But naturally there are resident pigs here, too. Born on Merrimajeel and most likely die to die there too.

At the time there was a very large black boar ranging Merrimajeel, first seen in early 1992. Stationhand Bill Pearson had seen it several times since then while mustering cattle in the lignum. While no pighunter, Bill knew a big 'un when he saw it and reckoned this particular boar was 'exceptionally large'. At any rate, as talk spread around the district to this effect then so did a number of pighunters go after the black boar, but each time he eluded them and their dogs. The boar had apparently killed several dogs.

Typically lambing time was bad news around Booligal and pretty much all over the west too. For instance, on Graeme and Sandra Headon's 'The Ville', a 30 000-acre run south of Booligal, large groups of boars, teaming up for the grand occasion, had accounted for up to 70 per cent of lambs in recent years.

Northeast of Hay, on Balaley station, ex-manager

Peter Tassell was out after pigs one night. Presently, the spotlight picked up a large black sow and six or seven piglets amidst a group of ewes about to give birth or having already done so. The sow ignored the sudden burst of brighter-that-day light, and curious what she would get up to the stationmen refrained from shooting. They watched the sow for about 10 minutes, in which time she went to one newly born lamb, too weak to stand, and killed it with one crunching bite, and as her piglets rushed to feed, she killed another lamb and then a third one. The sow of course was not only feeding her hungry youngsters but in the process was teaching them to hunt for themselves, all potential lambkillers.

It is amazing, Phillip says, how very little of a lamb is left when a pig has fed on it: the skin peeled back and as clean as a whistle, as though each bit of meat and fat and membrane has been carefully scraped off it, the meat all gone, the still-soft bones too, and all you usually found besides the pelt were the head and feet.

See that type of thing too often as you go around a lambing beat and it's difficult not to turn sour on feral pigs. It explains why Phillip Naughton, who has lived with pigs all his life, feels as he does when he says, 'So they not only affect lambing percentages very badly but they also root up land and hit fences like they're not there—especially old fencing. Then they lie in troughs in the summer and stock can't water there. Look, I don't want to share my environment with the pig if the truth is known. I'm very fortunate indeed that I have a reliable number of hunters to call on when their numbers build up: I expect that will happen as a result of all this rain.'

Rain?

You could only get into the station at that time in a four-wheel-drive vehicle and even then it was touch and go.

The hunters Phillip mentioned came, not surprisingly, from Melbourne. On an average weekend they reduced the pig numbers by between eight and ten pigs. The carcasses could be sold at Hay to cover costs and, mostly, to make a nice profit from one's sport.

From what Phillip said, he could trust these hunters. So they were not the type to kill stock, shoot up signs, drill holes in water tanks, leave a gate open. In all respects they conducted themselves so as not to upset the landowner. In return, they had the opportunity to enjoy top hunting whenever they came up here. Cuts both ways, right?

We walked away from the Lachlan River, passing under big river gum trees, Phillip attired as befitting a local sheepman in faded moleskins, blue cotton short, elastic-sided boots, all bearing the famous R.M. Williams tag. His hat was an Akubra.

About 70 metres from the homestead we pulled up short. There were the tell-tale tracks of a pig in the waterlogged earth.

Phillip fingered his freshly shaven jaw.' Hmm . . . pretty fresh, I'd say, wouldn't you?'

I nodded. 'Last night?' I suggested.

'Yes, last night.' He stared in a now pensive manner at the pig tracks, a medium-sized animal. 'Always be pigs here, you know.' He retreated into his own thoughts as we went on and I reflected on a little story he had told me earlier.

A good number of years ago Phillip owned a black-and-tan kelpie called Cassius, a grand little dog, game for anything. At night, next to the homestead, Cassius was chained to a kennel and also fed there. He only barked with good reason and so was an excellent watchdog. However, he started to bark for what seemed no good reason at all; moreover, it became a regular nightly thing, usually a short time after he had been chained up, which, because it was winter, was in the dusk. But each time Phillip rushed outside to see why his dog was barking there was nothing unusual to be seen.

In any event, this type of behaviour went on for about a month and one evening Phillip, unable to stand it any longer, stormed outside with every intention of whaling into Cassius once and for all. But much to his amazement, he saw the reason for his dog's barking: a large black sow was eating from the dog's bowl. The kelpie, unlike most dogs which wolf their food in the manner of their distant ancestors, much preferred to eat a little of his food and then retreat to his kennel, to contemplate a little, an hour say, and then devour the rest. The sow of course, no doubt seeing what she could forage on around the homestead in the initial stages, had come to recognise this pattern in the dog's behaviour and acted accordingly. And even Phillip Naughton, who has no fond feelings for feral pigs whatsoever, can, to his lasting credit, still raise a hearty laugh when he recounts that particular story.

14 The Commercial Aspect

I certainly see the role of commercialization in pest animal control; I think it is particularly important for pigs. I don't think eradication of the pig is feasible and so we have to look at how we're going to live with them in the long term and commercial use comes into that process in some way.

Jim Thompson, RLPB (Brisbane), talking with the author in Lakefield National Park, 1993

A light, almost misty rain was falling as bearded Russell Vivian weighed the carcass of a boar he'd recently taken delivery of at his wild game depot in Hay. The boar had come from a station north of Hay—saltbush country, up towards Ivanhoe.

'You picked a good time to come,' Russell said. 'This is about'—he gestured at the carcass—'as big as they get around here.' He leaned forward to check the weight on the scales: 113 kg.

The weight, I recalled, was the same as that of a boar John McManus and Brett McCahon had weighed in Lakefield National Park. There was, however, a basic difference in this particular case: that one had been live weight whereas the one Russell had just checked out was dressed out for human consumption.

It's worth noting that in the process of being dressed out in the field, which to meet regulations must be done within 15 minutes of the animal being killed, a pig will lose on average about a third of its live body weight. That being the case, this north of Hay boar would have had a live weight of around 140 kg, or about 308 pounds. Alive, he would have been a formidable customer for his tusks were big and, if not needle-sharp, as are those of many much smaller boars, they were still wicked weapons capable with one well-delivered blow of slashing a dog's jugular vein. Again, his battle-scarred shoulder shield, several inches thick, resembled a large slab: it was all hardpacked gristle no .22 calibre projectile would ever penetrate. It came as no surprise for me to learn

that the boar had been taken at night when he was perhaps at his most vulnerable—by a shooting party basically after roos but not averse to putting down such a boar which would net them around $113.

The boar's carcass, with particles of dried mud interlocked with the coarse hairs, was still claiming my attention when Russell said, 'Listen, I'll get Robert to give me a hand with it.' He grinned. 'I mean, you don't wanna get blood on that flash gear, do you?'

'You mean the stockman's clobber?'

'What else?'

'It's happened before,' I said matter of factly.

'Suppose so. Hang on, eh?' With that, he walked briskly towards a large shed.

As I waited there, I wondered just what sort of a life the boar had known. His had probably been a life of high adventure, with many dramas. Undoubtedly there had been quiet times too. Enjoyable times. I touched one of the dried bits of mud—like a hard nugget—and the thought came to me that this particular boar had taken his very last wallow.

Presently, Russell returned with a smiling young feller he introduced as Robert Martin. Like many young men in the country, Robert was into pigs in a real big way and while he would have chased them had there been no monetary gain associated with the sport, the added incentive of cold hard cash in his pocket made it doubly enjoyable.

In the field, Robert carried a carbine-length Winchester Model '94 in .30/30 calibre, arguably the most popular firearm/cartridge for pighunters in this country. He used two dogs: Major was a wolfhound cross built on gargantuan lines. Just a year old, he weighed 71 kg (to make sure, we weighed him in a woolsack; Major wasn't too impressed about that).

'Just wait till he really grows up,' Robert says gleefully; I'll bet the local pigs couldn't wait for that to happen.

Standing very much in big Major's shadow was Ginger—a spunky pit bullterrier. The dogs, Martin said, worked well together. They were both sensibly protected by neck collars and chest shields.

With some effort, the boar's carcass was taken to a big chiller, where eight or nine pigs had been hung up over the weekend just gone. Last Friday there had been about 40 pigs here and they had been picked up by truck as part of a consignment bound for Sydney, for Southern Game Meat.

The refrigerated truck, Russell said, had been chock-a-block with pigs, the majority of them coming from north of Hay—the Darling River system, around Cobar and Wilcannia.

'Yeah, it's a pretty big business,' Russell said, closing the heavy foor of the chiller behind us, 'and the way things are shaping up I expect it'll get a whole lot bigger yet.'

'But not as big as the roo industry?' Two hundred roo carcasses had come in overnight and the several men Russell employed to skin and bone them out, including Robert, were doing that right now. Out back, in two heaps, were over 7000 roo skins, the result of about seven or eight weeks work. So presently Russell was taking delivery of around a 1000 roo skins a week.

A rather wry smile crossed Russell's face as he replied:'Big as the roo industry? No, I don't expect it will.'

As already said, there are depots where wild game can be sold throughout the state; in fact, you'd be pushed to find anywhere in pig country where you couldn't sell a pig. Like other men in charge of these depots, Russell Vivian, while a kangaroo meat processor in his own right, is classed by Southern Game Meat, for instance, as an operator. A company printout explains the procedure once a hunter turns up with pigs to be sold:

Pigs are accepted into the box [chiller] after first being checked over and weighed. If any carcasses that arrive are in the opinion of the operator to be in doubt about their quality or as to how they have been shot then it is advisable to what we call T.B.A. them (To Be Approved) and payment is held up until the pig has been cleared through the system and if O.K. the operator is notified and payment is made.

Commission to operators is paid on a collective weight basis and this is paid less rejects. Rejects are decided by a Department of Primary Industries inspector when inspection is carried out in the boning plant. It is the responsibility of the box operator to then obtain the money paid out on a reject pig from the shooter to compensate the amount deducted from his commission.

The box should be kept hygienically clean and run on about 0°C—this can be varied to compensate for the outside temperature the box is standing in, e.g. winter or summer. The pig must be cooled as quickly as possible. A truck comes around on a regular basis and the operator supplies labour to load the truck. The blue copy of the load summary books is given to the driver of the truck which is given to the boning complex for checking the unloading.

At the present time in excess of 150 000 feral pig carcasses are exported each year, with an estimated value of around $15 million. The meat is sold primarily to France, Germany, and Austria, where it is marketed as 'wild boar'.

Significantly, Australia is the world's largest exporter of wild pig meat in the world and much higher levels of sustainable commercial harvesting are possible than prevail at the moment.

Let's consider a few facts and figures at this stage.

The wild pig—featured regularly in such local puplications as *Australian Sporting Shooter*, *Australian Gun Sports* and *Australian Shooters Journal*—is arguably Australia's foremost game animal. Editors of these magazines—John Downing (*Shooters Journal*), Ray Galea (*Sporting Shooter*) and John Robinson (*Gun Sports*)—know only too well that articles about wild pigs help to sell their monthly magazines.

So in Australia an animal which might cost the agricultural industry (collectively speaking) as much as $80 million, is, by the same token, the mainstay of a sporting and commercial enterprise in its own right that generates a huge financial turnover.

In Australia, then, pig hunting attracts on an annual basis somewhere between 150 000 and 200 000 people. They either shoot in a fully professional capacity, in a semi-professional situation, or simply for the sheer sport of it. Either way an estimated half a million wild pigs are killed each year in Australia. The meat industry believes that it could take delivery, without risk of oversupply, of 250 000 pigs a year, simply because the overseas markets are rarely, if ever, limited.

Precisely what in financial terms this many hunters inject into the economy is unclear, but C.A. Tisdell (1982) estimated it to be between $5 and $15 million. But whatever money is spent by pighunters, and all available evidence clearly suggests there are more people enagaged in pig hunting than there were a decade or so ago, one thing is absolutely certain: money spent on rifles, ammunition and other paraphernalia associated with hunting such as camping equipment, petrol and other running costs, on food and drink, on photographic items such as film and developing, is quite often spent where many people are hurting financially—that is, in small rural communities where a steady cash flow is essential to survival.

At the tiny Northern Territory settlement of Daly River I caught up with two fully professional pighunters: brothers Geoff (28), and Brett (26), were camped with an attractive young woman called Yvette (Brett's intended) in a roomy caravan near the river itself. Directly across the road from their well set-up camp was the local police station, appearing like an uncared-for relic of the lawless past. Also in sight was their chiller. They had put the carcass of an 86 kg boar in there last night. Numerous hawks with lazy wingbeats were hovering above the big metal container.

As a matter of interest, pigs oftentimes came into the township in search of melons. I was told in the hotel that several pigs had been seen recently standing outside the cop shop . . .

At any rate, the brothers Crowhurst came from a sheep station near Deniliquin in the Riverina; they knew the Hay area well. Right from being kids, Geoff said, they had hunted rabbits, foxes and, later, wild pigs. Pighunting was in their blood; there was nothing quite like it!

Out here, a long way from home, they had gained sole rights to a 100 000 acre block across the river— Aboriginal land. They paid the traditional landowners a mutually-agreeable royalty. Nothing for nothing, see.

The block, Brett explained, was good river country, a lot of rainforest stuff, pretty much like jungle, and endless small floodplains.

Floods?

Well, in early 1993, which set back the boys from the Riverina some, heavy rain had caused the Daly to rise 13 metres above the nearby crossing. Heli-musterers looking for stock in that country, which they reckoned resembled an inland sea, reported seeing mobs of pigs, getting thinner by the day, camped on small islands. Other pigs, miles from land,

with nowhere to go, appeared to be swimming aimlessly. Worse, some pigs were observed swimming out to sea—croc bait, was Geoff's succinct comment. But while the floods undoubtedly killed many pigs, professional hunting (as already indicated by Max King earlier) was still a viable proposition down the Daly.

Using .308 bolt-action Remington rifles, the brothers varied their hunting methods—either heading out at daybreak, in the evening, or spotlighting. Indeed, you had to diversify otherwise the pigs reacted by changing their habits—that is, hunt them long enough in the evenings and eventually they'd remain under cover until dark.

Geoff reckoned that several shooting parties on similar-sized blocks had pulled out of the game recently—not because pig numbers were too low but because the pigs had become much too cunning for them.

At the time they were shooting about 50 pigs a week and that, everything taken into consideration, gave them a good living. Nothing brilliant, you understand. The biggest boar they had taken here had a dressed-out weight of 130 kg. Their kills were collected every week to 10 days and trucked to Longreach in Queensland for Banner Game, out of Brisbane.

There are today over 300 domestic breeds or local varieties of pig scattered throughout the world. The entire pig population is approximately 750 million, with as many as 40 per cent in China. The former Soviet Union ranks second in pig production with the USA in third place.

Farmers all over the world raise pigs; the advantages of doing so are many. The meat is consumed in a variety of forms: chops, loin roasts, spare ribs, ham, bacon and sausage. Lard used for cooking is made of fat meat. Some religions, such as Islam and Judaism, strictly forbid the consumption of pork.

Tanneries process the skins of pigs into leather, which in turn is used to make clothing, saddles, watch bracelets, footballs, gloves, belts and shoes. The stiff hair of the pig provides bristles for brushes, and is used to stuff mattresses and baseball mitts and make insulating materials. Pig blood is used in the manufacture of fertiliser, animal feeds and medicines. The hoofs are used in making glue, the bones in manufacturing steamed bone meal, which, like animal feeds containing pig blood, is fed to cows, sheep, and pigs. Also, pharmaceutical companies use pig glands to make insulin and other medicines. As well as lard, pig fat is also made into soap, candles, salves, shaving cream, explosives and lubricating oils.

So virtually every part of the pig except its grunt is put to use. Such a broad diversity of uses must surely make the pig unique among domesticated animals and, significantly, a pig in fine condition harvested in the wild is in no way different from one reared behind a fence.

So is the feral pig of Australia an asset or a liability?

15 Drastic Measures

You could look across the swamps and see a mob of 150 pigs. A little further on there would be another 70; then no real distance beyond there you might run into 200 more.

Sue Jones, Quambone, talking about mustering on her grandfather's leased land in the Macquarie Marshes in the early 1970s

The herd of Hereford cattle resembled brown and white patchwork as they moved across a rolling, stump-clad paddock of perhaps a thousand acres. I've liked Herefords for a very long time and they made a real pretty picture with the cows mooching along and their calves trailing behind in a dutiful manner and it was all happening in a typically Australian landscape northeast of the spectacular Warrumbungle Mountains out near Coonabarabran in New South Wales.

It was early winter then, the days already short but mostly fine, with a cracker frost most mornings, and I was 18 years old and employed on the 10 000 acre property as a stationhand.

You know, I really loved it out there: loved the challenge, the country air, the sun on my face, the wind at my back, a top stockhorse to ride, and batching for myself in the shearers' roomy quarters where a nasty cold wind came in through gaps in the woodwork.

Distantly, I heard the boss call out in harsh tones to his dogs, then the sharp crack of his stockwhip, the barking of dogs, the bellowing of cattle that would rather stay right where they were. A day working cattle in the long shadow of the Warrumbungles all of 38 years ago.

Presently, I drew up on a rocky knoll, the landscape suddenly extended; the Warrumbungles as always arrested my attention. When I relaxed my grip on the reins, my black gelding, seizing the moment, dipped his head to feed on the coarse grass and I did not begrudge him doing that.

Some of the cattle started to drift towards me, spreading out from the main bunch we'd more or less grouped together and I stood up in the stirrups and, waving my hat, yelled out. That checked them, all right.

Suddenly, I saw movement in the tall, wheat-coloured grass over to my right and even further away from where the boss was. Something was running . . . something dark . . . It's a pig! I realised, the first one I had ever seen in a wild state. Breaking out of the grass and starting across bare ground, I saw a big, black and very hairy animal; I'd seen enough photographs of wild boar in the *Australian Outdoors*—very much a forerunner of the publications mentioned earlier—to know what it was.

With powerful lunging motions, as though grabbing at the ground with its front feet, the boar ran pellmell in the direction of what was the station's western boundary fence, all that separated it from the year-old sanctuary of what in 1955 had been gazetted as a national park. Quickly, the boar forced its way under a bottommost wire and vanished beyond a rise.

Presently the boss and I linked up at a gateway, through which the cattle, en route to the station headquarters, would go. I was still excited by what I had seen—bubbling over with it, in fact—and so I told the boss what I had seen and he nodded sagely and said there were quite a few of them in the ranges—he'd nodded towards the Warrumbungles—and that in the past—years ago—they'd had a lot of trouble with boars at lambing time but not so much in recent years. The boss fell silent then. He was over 70 years old, as hard as an ironbark tree, and he'd been on the place for over 50 years, settling there, I believe, with his wife soon after he was married.

'There's a lot more pigs north of here,' the boss went on, unusually talkative for once. 'Up around the Pilliga Scrub. Later, I would know the Pilliga

Ray and Neil take time out for grilled steak at old cattleyards.

Within the Macquarie Marshes (note the distinct reed line beyond the winter floodwaters).

Among a number of animals/birds found in the Macquarie are: *Left* Wedge-tailed eagle; *Right* Red kangaroo; *Below* Emus.

At Hay: Russell Vivian and the 113 kg carcass of a big
one from north of there

Above right: Ray Jones of the National Parks and
Wildlife Service in the Macquarie Marshes.

Right: The author in the Macquarie Marshes.

Between a rock and a hard place: Marty Maxwell in typical country near New Angeldool.

Left: Neil at an emu nestsite.

Below: A double-header for the author.

Scrub was the name for a vast region of semi-arid forest land. At this time, pigs were soon to start to increase their numbers in the Pilliga Scrub and by the late 1960s and early 1970s they were there in their many thousands, the place a mecca for pighunters from far and wide. The Pilliga Scrub.

With the kelpies urging them on, the cattle spilled through the gateway, the boss never taking his eyes off them as he said, 'Ever hunted pigs?'

'No, but I'd like to.'

'Well,' the boss said, 'the place to go for that is the Macquarie Marshes,' and he went on to explain they were northwest of the ranges. 'Pigs're so bad there at times,' he continued, 'that they just run cattle on some of the stations.'

You know, I can hear the boss saying all that to me as though it were yesterday and over the years it became an ambition of mine that I would visit the place he told me about all those years ago; but before that eventuated a great deal would happen in those marshlands and much of it was not good news for the feral pigs.

Situated about 500 kilometres from the coast, the Macquarie Marshes lie in the floodplain of the river bearing the same name. The marshes cover some 320 000 hectares of extremely level country and are basically divided into two main areas of semi-permanent swamp, several kilometres apart and linked by a narrow strip. The northern marshes in particular are heavily vegetated and virtually impassable in many parts; the southern regions of the marshes, however, are considerably more accessible.

The Macquarie Marshes were declared a sanctuary under the Birds and Animal Protection Act (1918–1930), today the Fauna Protection Act (1948). In 1971 18 000 hectares were designated a nature reserve under the management of the National Parks and Wildlife Service.

Importantly, the Macquarie Marshes represent the largest wetland refuge for birds in eastern Australia and about 189 species of birds frequent the area, of which 21 are known to breed there. An infrequent visitor is the magpie goose of the far northern regions.

While en route to the Macquarie Marshes in the winter of 1993, I considered it essential to the project to gain vital background information by talking with Terry Korn in Dubbo.

At the moment Terry is with the Department of Agriculture as team leader of a vertebrate pest control programme currently being implemented in the state. This, Terry says, involves working in close co-operation with the 57 Rural Lands Protection Boards spread around the state (in 1950 21 per cent of these boards reported feral pigs in their areas, but by 1977 the number had leaped to 91 per cent).

Terry Korn has been working with feral pigs—either in research or control—for 14 years now. Among the papers he has published on feral pigs is this relevant information:

The Macquarie Marshes are an important breeding and refuge area for the feral pig. During good seasons feral pig numbers increase and they foray onto neighbouring properties causing significant agricultural damage. During periods of drought the Marsh acts as a refuge area in which pigs can survive to re-populate the surrounding countryside following the breaking of the drought.

The impact of feral pigs on the flora snd fauna of Australian wetlands has not been quantified but reports by McKnight (1976), Giles (1978) and Tisdell (1984) suggest it could be significant when feral pig densities are high or during droughts, when there is fierce competition for available food and water.

Giles (1978) found that green vegetative material and roots form the bulk of the diet of feral pigs in the Marsh area. The most common herbs identified were *Medicago* sp., *Trigonella*, *Marsilea*, *Portulacca*, *Calandrinia* and *Tetragonia* spp. along with the rhyzomes of *Typha* and *Phragmites* sp. and *Paspalum paspaloides*.

A variety of fauna was also found in the gut contents including frogs (*Litoria* sp.; *Lymnodynastes* sp.), earthworms, insects and carcases of other large mammals such as sheep, cattle, pigs and kangaroo. A notable lack of bird remains was found in the stomach by Giles (1978) but this does not suggest that feral pigs have no impact on nest contents of ground nesting birds. Tisdell (1984) says that 30 per cent of Australian bird species nest on the ground and that their eggs and chicks risk being eaten by feral pigs, especially around water holes.

It's worth noting that by the late 1970s there might have been as many as 80 pigs per square kilometre in the Macquarie Marshes.

Obviously, Terry Korn said to me over a cup of coffee, drastic action had to take place against feral pigs in the Marshes. So what did happen there? Read this stuff, Terry said, handing me a sheaf of papers and I did.

Meeting of landholders, Pasture Protection Boards, the National Parks and Wildlife Service and Department of Agriculture resolved in 1980 that a control program based on poisoning with 1080 followed by regular aerial shoots from helicopters be implemented in an effort to reduce and then stabilise feral pig numbers at a relatively low level. Occasional burning of the dense reed beds was also included in the plan to improve the efficacy of the aerial shoots.

Recent preliminary field data suggest feral pigs consume about 1250 g of poisoned pellets. (P. O'Brien, personal communication). If this is the case then the poisoning programs would have killed approximately 11 000 feral pigs in and around the Nature Reserve.

Regular helicopter shoots utilising the NPWS aircraft began in January 1981. Up until October 1985 a total of 14 shoots of 3.8 hours or more have been conducted over the Nature Reserve (Table) resulting in the death of 6964 pigs. One of these shoots (November 1981) involved a commercial helicopter. Three deliberate burns were conducted; in August 1981, August 1984 and September 1985. Only the first and last burnt extensive areas. A wildfire in February 1981 burnt extensive areas of the Southern Marsh.

Month/Year		Pigs shot	Flying time (hours)	Pigs shot/ hour
1981	Jan	747	8.7	86
	Mar	487	8.1	60
	Aug	1240	9.8	127
	Nov	1038	31.2	33
1982	Oct	529	9.0	59
	Nov	232	5.0	46
1983	May	317	8.7	36
	Aug	184	4.8	39
	Oct	219	6.8	32
1984	Feb	74	3.9	20
	Aug	916	17.5	52
1985	Feb	84	3.8	22
	Jul	399	6.7	59
	Oct	498	7.1	71
Totals/ Averages		6954	130.9	53

As a result of all this control activity, sheepmen whose properties back against the Macquarie Marshes estimate feral pig numbers are today 10 per cent of what they were in the late 1970s.

As we shall read, regular helicopter control shoots still take place in the Macquarie Marshes, for it is very much as Terry Korn says:

> Besides having a time advantage over poisoning, helicopter shooting is also attractive because it is species specific, does not require either the removal of stock from treated areas or the worry that stock may gain access to bait stations. It can also be used in any seasonal conditions.

So there I was one particularly lovely Monday morning heading out of Dubbo—north—on the Mitchell Highway. On to Warren and then to Quambone.

Quambone?

Well, every town with a population in excess of 500 is claimed to be included in the *Reader's Digest Illustrated Guide To Australian Places* but, on that score, Quambone fails to measure up, which no doubt pleases what fulltime residents do live there.

In any event, Ray and Sue Jones had a small station on the outskirts of Quambone and had kindly invited me to stay with them. Ray worked with the NPWS as a field officer, and, specifically, he was in charge of feral animal control in the 18 000-hectare Macquarie Marshes Nature Reserve. In a recent telephone conversation, Ray said that he had been involved with helicopter shooting in the marshes and at present was carrying out a poison campaign aimed directly at foxes, because they were killing emu chicks.

With Warren behind me, I crossed the Macquarie River and instead of driving on to Gilgandra, I took a back road out past Haddon Rig sheep station and presently a small settlement came in sight—Quambone—and I wondered yet again in the light of how much control work had been done in the Macquarie Marshes on feral pigs just how many—if indeed any—I was going to see there?

16 Marshlands

Deep in the heart of the Macquarie Marshes the light was poor as Ray Jones and I skirted the clear-cut reedbed which separated the actual swamps from dry land. Ray paused and grinned tightly. There was sound reason for the predatory show of teeth: the wind was definitely in our favour as it swept across the grassy floodplains. The direction of the wind explained why there were in excess of a dozen pigs foraging out there in the open without any apparent concern.

We had spotted these pigs, or, rather, one at first, from Ray's department-issue vehicle: a 1993 Toyota flatdeck with just 13 000 km on the clock. At the time we were driving slowly along an embankment rising over a man-made channel and above the floodplain.

Using Pentax 8x42 fieldglasses, Ray had determined that the pig I had spotted was in fact a good-sized boar, and, moreover, there were a lot of pigs there. But when we'd set off on foot and soon cut the distance separating us by at least half, we knew that at least six of the pigs were adult males.

So now in the early dusk, we started the last leg of the stalk, moving away from the towering reeds, moving low to the ground and using whatever cover we could: a patch of tussocky grass, a tree that stood tall but was dead, taking no chances, doing it right.

Cupped in my hands was Ray's rifle: a lightweight custom-built .308 with a 4x Tasco scope. Ray had built up the weapon himself; the slim stock, fashioned of native timber, was especially appealing, and looking at it from a purely commercial aspect I thought that a great deal of largely untapped talent was wasted.

So because I was about to do the shooting, Ray was starting to hold back a little, letting me pick the route. Carefully, I moved to a deadfall, took several deep breaths, smiled at Ray as he snuck in alongside me, loving it.

Off again . . . what? . . . but it was just the sudden sound of pigs on the wind's cold breath. And it was cold. My wet pants were plastered uncomfortably to my legs because, earlier, I had stalked pigs through water in an attempt to photograph them at close range. I had succeeded, too. Just knew there were some fine photographs there—what was wet clothing compared to that?

A sudden angry grunt caused me to freeze!

Two males, both interested in the same sow, were sizing each other up like short-sighted gladiators. As though on cue they both reared up on hind legs and sparred for a few moments like arm-weary boxers going through the motions rather than really getting stuck into each other. The sow took no notice whatsoever of them.

When the two sparring partners dropped back to earth, the sow was already a little closer to us, sniffing at the ground. The bigger of the two boars lumbered after her and the other one turned away and at a trot headed for pastures new.

Close, now. Close enough to call the shots. Close enough for a skilled bowhunter to feel confident of hitting his mark, the arrowhead lodged behind the shoulder of the beast and deep enough to matter. That close. Indeed, it was remarkable how close to the pigs we were—none of them was further than 50 paces away, the previously mentioned sow and boar almost half that distance. And counting that particular boar, there were three adult males—two black and one a ginger colour—that appeared potential trophies. I drew a breath as I raised the .308.

Which one of the unsuspecting boars did I shoot at?

Two days previously I arrived at Ray and Sue Jones property—Boomanulla—in the late afternoon. They had owned the small run since 1976 and upon it ran sheep, a few cattle and chickens. Ray of course worked with the NPWS.

The Jones lived in an old-style dwelling, roomy and comfortable with a big open fire and it was, I thought, just like they were—totally unpretentious.

In her mid-thirties, Sue Jones grew up in Quambone. Her grandfather leased 2000 acres in the southern part of the Marshes, what they called a 'marsh block'. Sensibly, he ran cattle. Sheep? No, the country was basically too wet for them, and of course the pigs had to be taken into consideration. Pigs? Out mustering on her grandfather's block, young Sue cannot recall a time when she didn't see pigs out there, usually in their hundreds. Pigs in fact were all around Quambone. Pigs were a way of life around Quambone.

Ray Jones is ten years older than his wife, a compact, wiry sort of around average height. He looks like he's been around horses and sheep and cattle for long enough to count. The moment I met him I liked what I saw, the lean brown face, good cheekbones, the light blue eyes like washed-out denim. I also wondered who it was he reminded me of and, after a time, it dawned on me just who it was—the late actor, Steve McQueen. McQueen looked good wearing a broadbrimmed hat and holding a rifle in his hands, and Ray Jones was just like that, too.

That first evening at Boomanulla, after dinner, Ray, relaxing in an easy chair in front of a good fire, explained that while he was only too pleased for me to accompany him over the next couple of days while he went about his business, by the same token, I'd have to fit in with him.

'No worries,' I said. 'I was expecting that.'

Ray smiled at me as he raised his glass of beer. 'Good,' he said, and went on to say that while most of the poison work was done there were still two big blocks left to bait—one tomorrow afternoon and the other one the following day. Lending Ray a hand was Walgett-based Neil Teague, a ranger with the Rural Lands Protection Board. 'You'll like Neil,' Ray added, 'he's good value. We'll meet up with him at midday out there on the block. That'll give us a chance to have a look at the Northern Marshes in the morning: there's a trap set out there I need to take a look at.' Apart from checking out the pig trap, a large part of Ray's job was keeping a close watch on the 18 000 hectare nature reserve and the magnificent creatures that inhabited it.

Soon it was time for bed; Ray and Sue, country folk, got up early and went to bed early, too.

My sleeping quarters were located a short distance from the homestead, the type of basic but comfortable hut a stationhand might bunk in and be glad of. There were two beds in the single room, the beds made up, clean sheets, warm blankets, but I rolled out my swag and climbed into it in a mood of high anticipation. At long last I was about to visit the Macquarie Marshes. I could only hope the reality matched my preconception. Tomorrow and the next day would, all going to plan, tell the story.

Next morning, a Tuesday, dawned fine and clear, a light frost covering the ground. Such a glorious morning reminded me quite vividly of other winters' mornings when—not that far from here in a direct line—I'd worked beyond the Warrumbungle Mountains on a sheep station.

By eight o'clock we entered the nature reserve through a gateway Ray kept locked. We drove on with the sun at our backs, the dazzling rays spearing across the floodplains where the grass stood tall, profiling a lightning-blasted tree, highlighting the dense reedbeds so that they, like the grasslands, were glowing as though on fire.

Once across the northern bypass channel, built in 1968, we jolted along one of a number of raised tracks found in the reserve. I soon noticed some old cattleyards; they might, I thought, have stood there for a century.

'This is where Sue's grandfather had his block,' Ray explained, gesturing. 'See them yards? Well, Sue helped to build them when she was a kid.' So much for a hundred years old!

'When was that?'

'1974—I think.'

The year of the big floods, I thought.

Beyond the cattleyards, and to the north, there was a wondrous sight. Kangaroos on the move. They were streaming in single file along the edge of the reeds, flowing across the floodplain as though driven by the wind, weaving through the timber. Both red and grey kangaroos inhabit the marshes. These were red kangaroos, plains dwellers, the largest of all marsupials. I realised there were several hundred of them in sight, and, as though aware of what I was thinking, Ray nudged me with his elbow:

'You reckon that's a lot of roos?' He grinned. 'That's nothing! Just wait till this afternoon if you wanna see roos!'

Suddenly a big rangy tomcat streaked across the

track in front of the truck, a smaller cat just behind it. Pity Ray wasn't driving faster. Both cats vanished into a hollow tree, and, cats being cats, the only way you'd get them out of there would be by burning it.

Like all true bushmen, Ray Jones hates feral cats. With an angry shake of his head, he said, 'One good thing about the bait we're putting out is that it's the right strength to nail cats, too.'

'What about pigs?'

Ray just shook his head.

Presently, we turned about and started back to the cattleyards, a rather shabby-coated fox running off through the tall grass, pausing once to look back, then off again, tail streaming behind it.

With the cattleyards in sight, Ray said the trap he'd baited wasn't that far away from here. When had he baited it?

'Last Friday,' he admitted. Four days ago. 'Should've been back before now but with one thing and another . . .' his voice trailed off. Then: 'I put a blind roo in it.'

'Hope it was dead.'

'As only a .308 slug can make it,' he said drily.

Well, there was a pig in the trap—a black boar weighing about 40–50 kg. He appeared quite demented as he eyed us through the wire bars of his prison; there was very little left of the roo—just a big hip bone and some mangled skin. A shot rang out, hard and flat; Ray had ended the boar's undoubted despair.

Together, we dragged it out of the trap. Ray dressed it out. The carcass was dumped without ceremony in the back of the Toyota; Ray would sell it in Quambone, the proceeds being used for the upkeep of the nature reserve. Sensible, that.

Which of course left the steaming guts and other unwanted parts spread over the ground near the trap. Would Ray re-bait the trap with this? He shook his head and explained that they had tried baiting traps with dead pigs on several occasions and that it hadn't worked. 'They won't even go near a trap that's got their own kind in it,' Ray finished. That, I thought, revealed a sensitive side to a wild pig's nature; something to admire.

'Maybe they would in extraordinary circumstances,' I pointed out.

He raised an eyebrow. 'Turn cannibal, you mean?'

'Yes.'

'So do we,' Ray Jones said.

The sun was well up by now and we hadn't driven very far when we saw pigs. They were feeding close to the reeds, out where the grass was vividly green and isolated pools of water reflected the sun like huge windows in a skyscraper.

'Pretty good boar amongst them,' Ray summed up with the aid of his Pentax fieldglasses. 'Hmmm . . . could be as many as nine or . . . ten there.' A pause and then, 'Shit! They're off!' The pigs ran hard and soon merged with the cover. One boar looked especially big. 'That was the biggest pig I've seen here in quite some time,' Ray went on, quite excited about it. 'Sure like to see him hanging on the scales in town.'

'Not about to happen, Ray.'

'It might when a chopper comes in again,' Ray pointed out realistically.

I digested that with all the appetite of a vegetarian faced with a greasy pork chop. Helicopters! Unlike a Colt revolver, which was said to make all men equal, the use of a helicopter, by far the most versatile airborne machine yet devised, gives man a decided 'edge' in his unending battle to control feral animals.

'When's the next chopper shoot?' I asked.

'In the spring,' Ray replied.

'I'll bet the pig can't wait!'

Again we spotted pigs—four small ones foraging in swampy ground bisected by winding streams; it was, I suppose, really an extension of the marshlands. We watched them for a few minutes; they were almost continually moving. Then I sneaked in on them with a photograph in mind, easy enough with the wind right, but no joy whatsoever when I had to cross one, and then another, thigh-deep waterway. The water was like pure ice.

On my return to Ray, who grinned at my obvious discomfort, I mentioned that all but one of the pigs was spotted. He nodded. Apparently this was a common-enough occurence in the Marshes—as, for that matter, were striped piglets. Ray told me that many of the pigs grew a dense underfur in winter, just like the European wild boar. I mentioned that in cold climates the Asian pig did the same thing, and there have been reports of pigs in the Cape Tribulation region, north of Cairns, with the same type of coat; although what they would need a woolly undergarment there for poses a question. Again, Ray said, he had seen many pigs in the Marshes with a definite cheekstripe and that was typical of the European wild boar, wasn't it? True, I agreed, but the same thing could be said of a number of subspecies of *Sus scrofa* found in the Pacific regions. However, given the geographical location of the Macquarie Marshes, and the fact that the first pigs that went bush here would have almost certainly been of European, rather than Asian, stock, Ray's theory that the pigs here were a throwback to the European wild boar was most likely correct.

Still talking about piglets—well—those we had just seen were not yet past that early stage. Ray judged they were aged between three and four months. So what were they doing on their own?

Ray's explanation made sense. A helicopter shoot had taken place here two months ago. Typical of such shoots was the fact that when a shot was fired at an adult animal, the small ones, like well trained survivalists, tended to scatter instantly. They were also the last ones to be shot at in a group of pigs which, for instance, might contain three or four adults and several half-grown pigs. Moreover, when a shooter did try and nail a little one, it usually proved an elusive target. So some piglets, and oftentimes many, escaped helicopter shoots.

So if Ray was correct in his assumption as to what had happened in this particular instance—that is, the four little pigs had lost their mother to a helicoper shooter two months previously—they had been on their own from a very early age. Perhaps a month or two at the most. During the past three months the weather had often been bitterly cold in the Marshes and much wetter than normal. Moreover, there were predators about: foxes lurking surreptitiously in the tall grass or moving stealthily through the scattered river red gums, and wedge-tailed eagles on high, but never so high that their superb eyesight couldn't spot such a delectable morsel (in areas where both pigs and eagles are plentiful it is not uncommon, by searching under the nest of an eagle, to find the skull and bones of piglets and even smallish pigs lying there with whatever else the adult birds have fed the chicks with). So when you take everything into consideration a logical question is what other ungulate at such an early age could survive in this situation? None, I think, but the offspring of *Sus scrofa*.

Afoot, we walked slowly and alertly through the scattered trees—the river box, the acacias, the always lovely gums. In a channel, like small sailboats, were two white pelicans and two black swans; the swans had all the grace of a ballerina. Ray's memory was jogged by the sight of the swans because he told me

he'd once seen a black sow actually in the process of raiding the nest of a black swan. It had been in the western side of the reserve, mostly red gum country. The sow had already devoured one of the two eggs the nest had contained and the other one, partly eaten, was still in its mouth when Ray shot it.

'That type of thing probably happens more than we realise, Ray finished.' I expect he was right about that.

Presently, we came to the actual Macquarie River. It was narrow and deep at this point and several roos that had fled before us were now crossing it. They swam in the manner of dogs, paddling with their short front arms. Unlike pigs, however, they have no real staying power in deep water.

In 1990 serious flooding occurred in the northern part of the reserve and untold numbers of roos found refuge from the deep floodwaters on small islands. By the time the floodwaters receded an estimated 4000 roos had died in that situation. The ripening carcasses lured many pigs, and rangers and field staff, aware of the fact, seized the opportunity to kill a great number.

That afternoon I drove Ray's vehicle around a huge block while Ray and Neil Teague baited it for foxes. Kangaroos? There were thousands of them out there, including two albino red kangaroos. Also there were hundreds of emus. While the boys weren't concerned about pigs taking the eggs of an emu, saying they were too hard for them to break, Ray did admit that only recently he'd come across some broken eggshells that, by the sign around them, made him strongly suspect pigs were responsible.

Ranger Neil, a rangy six-footer with blond hair and a drooping moustache right out of the mid-1970s, was directly concerned with feral animals and worked with graziers who had problems with them, which, Neil said wryly, was just about everyone who owned or managed a station in his massive area of responsibility that stretched from here in the Marshes to the Queensland border—about six million acres all up, Neil reckoned.

Later, in the evening, with the day's work done, we drove around in search of pigs. Saw some too. Neil and I took one apiece, Neil using a .222 and me Ray's .308. No big deal since we were standing on the back of the vehicle at the time. The boar I shot— while small—would have been a real handful for dogs to cope with because his tusks, pencil-thin and honed to perfection, would have cut and slashed them to bits.

Next morning we were up with the birds and away before they'd decided just what to have for breakfast. With four hours at our disposal before we would again meet up with Neil to complete the poison operation (which I shall not comment on any further), we intended to make every single minute count. And we did: we saw a number of pigs—including a good sort of tan-coloured boar, and, later, several groups of piglets lacking adult supervision. They were about the same size as those I had seen yesterday, and they too were in good condition. Roos? Yes, they were almost always in sight: thousands of roos, more roos that you could shake a stick at. To me it seemed like some serious culling should take place here and, when I said as much to Ray, he made no comment. Fair enough because he worked for the NPWS and culling native animals in a nature reserve is not in line with their policy. Still with roos—one old man roo we startled was so badly crippled up with rheumatics he could hardly hop.

'Poor old bugger,' Ray said.

'He won't last long,' I said, watching the old fellow come to such a lopsided halt it was a wonder he didn't topple over.

'You're right,' Ray agreed. 'He won't see the winter out.'

Particularly interesting was the number of pig nests we encountered: big grassy beds in sunny, sheltered locations, and we even came across nests in the lignum: the pigs tunnel into it and clear a large area of the interior, often lining it with grass. I crawled into one such nest and found it lovely and warm in there and could, I thought, have easily stretched out and had a doze. On second thoughts that would have made no sense at all: there are 15 known species of snake living in the Marshes and, in winter, you never quite knew where they were hibernating. Although common sense said it wasn't anywhere near where a pig lived!

Dusk . . .

Soundlessly, Ray Jones moved in behind me as I pondered which of the three boars, all within shooting range, I should take. Sensing my dilemma, Ray sidled even closer and breathed into my ear, 'That one.' Half turning, I saw that his slit-eyed gaze was focused on the nearest and obviously biggest boar. Nodding, I raised his .308 rifle, it came up smoothly. I aimed, touched the trigger, and, as flame spurted out of the muzzle, willed the round home. The projectile hit hard and hit true. Down went the boar.

Pandemonium!

With my blood racing, I lined up on another likely looking black boar running across my line of vision. Fast? I'll say he was moving fast. I fired at this one as though I were using a shotgun and it was a bobbing rabbit I was aiming at. The best thing to do under the circumstances. He too went down to a heart shot.

A trophy boar, with tusks to equal my Arnhem Land boar?

No, not this time.

17 Border Country

Woollerbilla Station, Southeastern Queensland

Here in the black soil country in the far-flung watershed of the 320 kilometre-long Culgoa River, professional hunting guide, Marty Maxwell, pulled up alongside a dam.

'Take a look at this,' he said, switching off the ignition.

We got out of the twin-cab Toyota to a lovely early afternoon in late winter, the day warm to hot, the sky clear, the Border Country.

In the open, utility-like back of the vehicle, Eric and Bear, both out of the same mother, a pedigree bullterrier, watched us with typical canine interest. As yet they hadn't had a run after pigs but, from the confident way Marty was talking about his prized hunting concession near Hebel, it was only a matter of time before hard action started on 22 000-acre Woollerbilla station.

On the hard-baked rim of the dam, Marty lighted a tailormade smoke and explained this dam was called Pig Tank; there were no prizes on offer for guessing why. In any event, Pig Tank was dry. There were a couple of dead cattle in the middle of the dam, some sheets of rusty corrugated iron: an eyesore in the bush, all right. The mandatory windmill was there of course—hell, it might have been there when Kidman rode through this country.

Marty hunkered down on his heels, pulling on the weed.

'This is the place I told you about yesterday; figured you'd like to see it.' He tipped the wide brim of his Stetson lower over his eyes.

'Where they dug for water, y'mean?'

'Yeah.'

So this dried-up dam was where in times of drought—and a two and a half yearspell without rain had only recently broken—the pigs came to. In the middle of the dam they dug down through the clay and silt for several metres causing small pools of water to form—not much, but enough to suffice them until the rains finally came and the brown land was, if only for a short period of time, tinged green. The land was like that now, tinted with green.

'Yeah, they're true survivors and no mistake,' Marty said, straightening. A big man is Marty Maxwell, about six feet tall and over 100 kg. He then added that the holes the pigs dug resembled mineshafts and were so steep-sided that the dogs refused to go down them even if they were very thirsty. 'Let's go find them pigs I've been telling you about.' He dropped the butt of his cigarette and stamped it out.

I raised my eyebrows. 'Telling me about? Bragging about, more like.'

'Yeah'—he grinned—'that too.'

The dogs looked happy when we climbed into the cabin of the vehicle and were no doubt even more so when the Toyota started up with a gutsy roar and Pig Tank was left behind to the sole attention of a couple of crows that had greeted our arrival with raucous cries.

And so we went on through that always interesting country. The property, Marty explained, had recently changed hands and at present wasn't carrying any stock. This was cattle country, of course.

And so as the landscape unfolded and the roos ran through the timber and the birdlife was almost always evident, the pleasing voice of Garth Brooks was keeping us company as he told about the stirring exploits of a Texas Ranger and the song seemed in keeping because we were in hard border country too.

Marty Maxwell operates his guided hunting venture—Narran River Safaris—out of New Angeldool. In the 1880s, Angeldool, north of Lightning Ridge and practically on the Queensland border, boasted five hotels, a hospital, a Cobb & Co. waystation, and a population of several thousand

On Kilberoo station they know all about wild pigs!

New Angeldool is just down the track to the left . . .

Keith Roberts at Yantabulla station.

The old hotel at Hebel.

Joe Geiger is sent crashing to the ground.   He keeps the pig at bay by using his feet.

He somehow regains his footing and holds the animal at arm's length.

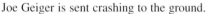

people. Today, New Angeldool is the next thing to a ghost town, bypassed by the unsealed road heading to the Queensland border. Perhaps a dozen familes live in New Angeldool today and because there is no store, petrol station or school here they are frequent visitors to Lightning Ridge, about 48 kilometres away.

But New Angeldool suits the people who do live there and that goes for Marty and Kellie Maxwell; indeed, Kellie, an attractive blonde, told me that her family (Barrett) had had a long association with the region, and the house I stayed in with them had been in the family since the late 1880s.

In any event, I had arrived at the Maxwells' old stone dwelling the previous day. Come mid-afternoon, the dogs had jumped with eagerness into the back of the Toyota and Marty, clamping a big Stetson on his head, had said he'd see her later, to Kellie, and we'd taken off in ideal weather to nearby Bodha station—an Aboriginal-owned property of 70 000 acres upon which they run 5000 merino sheep.

As well as pigs of trophy potential, there were many feral goats on the station, some, Marty said, carrying 40-inch racks, a prime target for both local and overseas hunters.

Presently, we came to what Marty said was a 'big rough paddock with lots of hard country in it'.

How big? I asked.

About 10 000 acres, he replied.

And as for 'hard country', well, what I was seeing on Bodha station looked remarkably like the terrain around Lightning Ridge or at Coober Pedy in South Australia—only fit for drilling holes in. It made you wonder how the sheep made out.

At a big, near-overflowing dam, Marty, stopping the vehicle, explained that this was the only water in a radius of perhaps five miles. A year ago, knowing that several big boars were in the habit of watering here, he had brought a client to the dam with the intention of simply waiting—a time-proven method for hunting success in such dry country—for pigs to turn up in the evening to water.

Back then—winter—the country was still in the grip of drought. Feed was so scarce in that crippled landscape that a lot of sheep had died before the manager of the station, Rex Skuthorpe, had made arrangements to lay out oats around the dam. The pigs, Marty reckoned, probably thought that was one helluva good idea.

So the 29-year-old hunting guide and his client, both armed with scoped rifles, had sat down on a stony ridge in the shade of trees with a commanding view of the dam and most of its surrounds. In time, pigs started to appear. They saw several sows with young, watched them water, watched one sow feeding on the scant remains of a sheep, saw others searching for, and locating, oats.

No boars, huh, the client said with a doubtful shake of his head. Give it time, Marty replied, knowing that it was very often late before the big fellows came to water.

Evening started to close in around them, and you realised with a shiver how very cold it could be in the Border Country. About then it happened: two black boars appeared—more or less backing out—from a patch of scrub not that far away. Each boar was holding a part of a dead lamb.

The client, sucking in his breath, started to raise his rifle but Marty clamped a hard hand on his wrist.

'Wait!' Marty whispered.

Soon fascinated by what they saw, they watched the boars pulling hard on the carcass, and the remarkable thing was that no matter how hard they yanked and pulled the carcass remained intact. Then, as though tiring of this macabre tug-of-war, the boars dispensed with the carcass and attacked each other, making maddened sounds as they slashed at each other's well-protected chest and shoulder regions.

The battle was still going on over the dead lamb when two well-aimed shots rangs out. One boar dressed out at 105 kg, and the other 80 kg. As Marty Maxwell says, you remember things like that.

Another interesting story Marty told me concerned a black boar that lived close enough to New Angeldool to be considered a resident. While ranging up and down the Narran River via wellworn pads, the boar invariably camped in a big patch of tall lignum on the north bank of the river, about 200 metres from where Bobby Barrett (Marty's father-in-law) lived.

For six months they knew that the boar was there and for six months, sometimes every single weekend in sequence, Marty, to whom the boar soon became an obsession, tried to catch it with his dogs, oftentimes his brothers-in-law, Ben and Shannon, getting in on the act too.

But in such thick lignum the boar beat them every single time they went after it, hearing or smelling them in plenty of time. To escape from the dogs the boar normally took to the river, crossing it so quickly that in most instances, Marty thinks, it was on the far side and off before the dogs even thought about entering the water.

One day, Marty Maxwell decided on another ploy: they would leave the dogs behind. So with Ben and Shannon, each man armed with a 12-gauge shotgun and a load not designed for feathered game, he entered the lignum. It was impossible to move quietly in there but he reckoned they had the wind right and that was always more important.

With stealth, Ben parted the thick growth in front of him and spooked the boar which took off with an almighty 'woofing!' sound which at such close range was just about frightening enough to scare any pighunter. The boar more or less ran into the path of Shannon, who, like Marty, was at a 50-metre distance from his brother. Shannon fired instinctively and the boar went down. A big black boar that had really troubled no one in New Angeldool.

Dressed out, the boar tipped the scales at 90 kg, and his tusks were long and very sharp and so it was just as well, Marty reflects, that neither Eric nor Bear, who were very young then, had managed to pin the boar down to a physical confrontation. Nevertheless, Marty Maxwell, like so many pighunters, knows all about the trauma of losing a good dog in the field of battle.

Born and bred on his folks' sheep station at Wee Waa, near Narrabri, in the wheat-growing belt of New South Wales, he grew up in country fringing the famed Pilliga Scrub. Hunting pigs for the likes of Marty's Dad and his mates wasn't just a pleasant weekend jaunt, it was a form of survival.

So Marty's father and his station friends, all with a common cause in mind, would saddle their horses, gather their dogs about them, and head out towards, or even into, the Pilliga Scrub.

Later on, when Marty was still young, he would go out with the menfolk, too. And he, like they, like many thousands of Australians living in country areas, soon fell under the mesmerising spell of the ancient sport of kings and noblemen.

Of the many dogs he would own, and that now covers 25 years, Marty best remembers a black-and-white sheepdog/cattledog cross. He called it Dog. Why? Well, at the time of having to pick a suitable name for it, all he could think of was how very much the pup reminded him of Murray Ball's lovable creation in the comic strip, Footrot Flats, and so 'Dog' it was.

Like that fictitious Kiwi border collie, Aussie Dog,

out of Wee Waa, was clued-up, too. Yes, Dog was super smart and much too nimble-footed to ever get himseld in a nasty predicament with a boar . . . or was he?

On the day in question, Marty was also using a bullterrier/cattledog cross, and his good mate Peter Bullen had with him a fine cattledog which many think, and they have their reasons, make the best pigdogs of all.

They were hunting in plains country where wheat and turnips really attracted the big pigs, the wheat of course definitely packing on the kilos.

At any rate, it was Peter's cattledog that actually spooked the boar, a huge spotted pig with instant mayhem uppermost in his enraged mind.

When Marty came running up, the ruckus had already started. He heard his bullterrier cross scream and then saw it pitchforked high into the air, over the boar's back. It came down so limply that Marty knew it was dead before it hit the ground. Not content with that the boar, before making good its escape, took out Dog. Took him out badly. As badly as it gets. There were deep gashes to Dog's chest and shoulders, and a particularly deep cut in his throat. Dog died soon after.

'You know,' Marty says sorrowfully today, 'we never used any protective gear in those days—no collars or chest shields, nothing at all.'

This, then, is just a little sample of Marty Maxwell's background before he became a professional hunting guide several years ago.

Today, there are many hunting guides like Marty Maxwell and Max Davidson operating in Australia who, among other game, offer pig hunting. Similarly, there is an ever-growing number of stations, mostly at this stage in New South Wales, catering for pig hunters too. Right, a lot of station people have come to realise that their feral pigs are valuable animals in their own right, and that they can be a resource rather than a liability. On many stations that offer what we might term 'pig hunting holidays' there is accommodation and, if required, a guide. No matter if the guide is a stationhand rather than a seasoned professional hunter, for working on the place he knows where the pigs are. In hunting circles that's called 'local knowledge'.

Personally, I see a great future for the exploitation of wild pigs both by professional hunting guides and people on the land. Taking everything into consideration, I see it as a good thing too. An address list and locations of professional hunting guides and stations that offer pig hunting appear in the appendixes.

Woollerbilla station . . . an hour or so later.

With a dark scowl, Marty Maxwell looked with contempt at the small pig Eric and Bear had run down. He prodded the lifeless animal with the toe of his boot, and then with an expression of disgust, said, 'They're doing their very best to embarrass me, y'know.'

I could well sympathize with the man: twice, now, we'd spotted a mob of pigs running through the timber and each time we'd given chase on foot, and on both occasions the dogs had nailed a very small pig.

'Maybe there wasn't a boar with them,' I offered in a conciliatory fashion.

'Maybe not but'—and Marty glared at his dogs—'even if there were, then these two gutless bastards wouldn't wanna know a bloody thing about it.' Eric and Bear looked up at their irate master and they were not smiling. 'Ah, shit,' Marty went on, 'let's get on with it!' He strode off through the bush. The dogs slunk after him.

Back at the vehicle, Marty took time out for a smoke. Resting up against the dusty tailgate, we busted open a can of soft drink apiece. Mighty hot yakka running through the bush like silly buggers chasing pigs on Woollerbilla station.

We drove on in the mid-afternoon, the weather turning cloudy, sultry. One sandy track merged with another and I thought it was just as well one of us knew where we were going. Now and them we'd startle roos and emus . . .

In well scattered timber, Marty Maxwell and his dogs ranged a little ahead of me. Suddenly, Marty stiffened—he'd seen something. But what? My eyes flashed to the dogs but they were far from excited. At that moment, perhaps 60 metres away, there was movement in the shade of some trees and a number of red kangaroos stood up, stood tall so they could sum up the situation, and, having done so, turned about and moved away in slow, lazy bounds. Marty, lowering his rifle, smiled a little ruefully.

Almost immediately, the roos still in sight, two good-sized pigs were running from left to right across our line of vision. Semi-crouched, rifle at the ready, Marty followed their rapid, bobbing progress with the muzzle of his rifle. But he was unable to see them properly because of a patch of scrubby growth, and as enough mistakes had already been made today, he snapped at me:

'Boar?'

'No!' I shot back.

Marty held fire as the two sleek sows bolted into the start of what appeared through the thinning trees to be a considerable stand of lignum.

Marty gestured. 'Usually get onto them here. Great place for boars—they really like this 'soft' country.'

'Did Tony get his boar here?' Tony Pizzata was a top feature rifle with the *Sporting Shooter* magazine and, only recently, he had hunted with Marty and ended up with a fine trophy boar.

Marty shook his head. 'No—it was near the dam I took you to yesterday—y'know, where the two boars were fighting over a dead lamb.' He paused. 'Wouldn't mind running into a boar like that again.'

Here in the lignum we started to come across a lot of sign, and there were many game trails used of course by all that resided here. There was also a strong sense of urgency about the dogs. Maybe they were about to redeem themselves in their master's eyes.

All of a sudden, almost shocking in impact, a black boar exploded out of low cover away to our right. He ran hard on a diagonal course, kicking up black earth. In the few seconds he was in plain sight I noted his build: all chest and shoulders, the hindquarters of a hyena. I judged he would weigh between 70 and 90 kg.

Almost immediately the dogs went after it and Marty, perhaps afraid that he might shoot one of them rather than the boar, or perhaps because it was too fast for him, didn't shoot.

We could have been in for a long, hard chase and that was something I didn't relish the idea of but, much to my surprise, the boar was bailed within 50 metres; and so when Marty and I, shoulder to shoulder, burst onto the scene the dogs were holding it and the boar was screaming and Marty thrust the Ruger into my hands and withdrawing a wicked-looking knife from a sheath at his waistbelt stepped in quickly behind the boar and ended it all there and right then with cold steel.

'Top boar!' Marty cried with delight as he examined the boar's tusks. Yes, there was very reason for his jubilation: they were magnificent tusks, unblemished because of the 'soft' nature of the country the boar inhabited, and perhaps because he was careful of his weapons. Either way, I had not seen a finer set of tusks anywhere.

'Good dogs!' Marty praised. 'Good dogs!' He fondled them.

Right, Eric and Bear, showing their teeth and

batting their tails on the ground, had made good their earlier mistakes in the best possible way.

'This calls for a drink,' Marty said.

'My shout,' I said, quite looking forward to visiting the old hotel at Hebel.

Marty grinned. 'Won't argue about that.'

Eric and Bear were still grinning like crazy.'

18 Back o' Bourke

Listen, there are over 300 sheep stations in this district and every single one of them has problems with feral pigs!

Ranger Richard Atkinson, RLPB, Bourke

Blink twice and you just might miss Fords Bridge on the Warrego River northeast of Bourke. Still, Richard Atkinson, the local Rural Lands Protection Board troubleshooter, had reckoned there wasn't much to the place when we'd spent some time together yesterday in Bourke.

And yet Fords Bridge was interesting to me inasmuch as Andrew Simms' Green Creek station was located here. The 55 000-acre property is a mixture of red country (which doesn't flood) and black country (which most certainly does).

On Green Creek, the RLPB boys had shot, trapped and poisoned so many pigs over a long period that eventually they were of the opinion they had eliminated them completely there. Stationfolk agreed with them. There was no sign of pigs anywhere.

Then just a matter of a few weeks before I passed through Fords Bridge a number of sheep were destroyed on Green Creek station by RLPB personnel because of a suspected footrot outbreak. They shot 40 sheep initially. In less that a week, Richard Atkinson admits wryly, they had all been cleaned up by pigs.

Still further northwest of Bourke is Yantabulla. It is the name of a station and also a telephone exchange. Yantabulla became a 43 000-acre station when Keith and Nora Roberts took it on in 1968; the telephone exchange was there before then. At Yantabulla, en route to Hungerford, on the New South Wales/ Queensland border, I had 'smoko' with Keith and Nora Roberts. They made me most welcome.

Born in Bourke, Keith found work as a stationhand on Nellyvale, another property in excess of 40 000 acres, in 1955. The early-to-mid 1950s—following the big flood of 1950—saw a huge increase in pigs back o' Bourke. Nellyvale was a case in point. Two shearers who were there for a month went out hunting each weekend and shot over 600 pigs using .22 rifles.

But it was what happened during the drought of '57 that Keith Roberts remembers best about pigs on Nellyvale. Typically many sheep bogged in tanks— hopelessly trapped as though in deep quicksand, easy prey for the likes of dingoes, eagles and crows that pecked out their eyes. Prey for pigs, too. They would, Keith says, rip out a sheep's stomach while it was still alive. A particularly graphic incident is forever stamped on Keith's mind. He had ridden out to one such tank where a lot of sheep had been killed by pigs. As he'd drawn near, a big old boar had moved away with reluctance from what Keith had presumed was a dead sheep, its intestines spread about. But when he stepped down from his horse, Keith realised that the sheep wasn't dead at all—its exposed heart was still beating. The sheep might have been waiting for a sickened young stationhand to end its untold misery, and whether that was the case or not, a .22 rifleshot rang out.

'Pigs?' Keith Roberts says today. 'I hated their guts for doing that kind of stuff and I still do.'

Leaving Yantabulla, I presently came to Sandy Point station. Good name. This was red sand country where the station's mail was collected at the side of the road, and while a big red roo was standing at the gateway to the property I doubt very much if he was on the payroll as a boundary rider.

I was now very much in what is called the Cuttaburra Basin. Before large-scale helicopter shoots took place here, this was a terrible place for pigs; they were as numerous and as troublesome as anywhere in the country. Lambs? You'd be lucky if 20 per cent survived. On Kilberoo pigs simply took over the water troughs, wallowing in them during the heat of the day, stopping the cattle, milling around in distress, from watering there. So you did what you had to: you shot or chased off the pigs, emptied and cleaned the troughs, refilled them, and then stood on guard duty while the desperately thirsty cattle drank their fill. Do that type of thing day in day out in century-plus temperatures and life as they say sure did get mighty tedious. Pigs? Yes, they hated them on Kilberoo too.

A chance for a revenge of sorts came with the massive floods of 1974, when much of the basin of the Cuttaburra River resembled a huge inland sea and the pigs swam to whatever high country they could find: isolated red islands. Stationfolk used boats to reach the stranded pigs and, on Sandy Point and adjoining Kia Ora, they shot over 2000 pigs, as many as 400 on one small island.

Much of course would change in the Cuttaburra Basin once feral pig eradication shoots took place using helicopters. The result of one such shoot—spread over three days in October, 1987—can be seen below:

Property	Flying hours	Result
Kilberoo and SandyPoint	7	1600 Pigs
Kia Ora	2.5	300 Pigs
Rosedale	2.5	300 Pigs
Clifton Downs	5	650 Pigs
Killawan	2	300 Pigs
Phora	1	150 Pigs
	20 hours	3300 Pigs

In this particular operation, four experienced shooters were involved using semi-automatic 12-gauge shotguns and .308 calibre rifles. Total ammunition expended was approximately 4980 00/SG shotgun cartridges and 400 rounds of .308. Yet despite such high kill figures it was considered, in the aftermath of this shoot, that there were still thousands of pigs ranging the six stations in question.

On Kilberoo and Sandy Point, for instance, which obviously carried a much higher pig population, the shooters found it physically impossible to load, aim and fire at all the pigs sighted; moreover, the pilot, Tim Turner out of Mungindi, was unable to stay with the sheer numbers of pigs—in mobs of 30–50 they were coming across one after another. Then on Kia Ora the pigs were able to conceal themselves in heavy lignum.

Richard Atkinson, who participated in this and other similar helicopter shoots, told me it was surprising how few big boars were sighted from the air and yet, as they all well knew, they were there, all right. But one particularly big boar was taken in the far-flung Bourke district during this period. It was shot, Richard says, in the middle of nowhere, somewhere between Bourke and Cobar. It dressed out at 140 kg (over 180 kg on the hoof), and its tusks—14 centimetres of very sharp ivory—protruded out of its lower jaw. You could have nightmares over a boar that size, Richard says with feeling.

In the Bourke district, Richard believes that helicopter shoots on a regular basis are the best possible way of keeping pigs in check. Not that he is looking forward to the next shoot. Helicopter shooting, he says, is no joyride: cramped in the back of a Hughes 500 with another shooter (and 'cramped' is right, for Richard stands over two metres high) as the machine swings from one side to the other, the men shooting alternately. The noise factor, for one thing, was horrendous after a while, and so was the October heat, an oven-like blast to remind you that summer was just around the corner. Worst of all was the recoil of the shotgun, thump-thumping against your shoulder, banging against your jaw until it throbbed, even rattling the teeth inside your head after an hour of it. Richard Atkinson once shot 240 pigs in one hour but, as he admits, he was physically and mentally shattered at the end of it.

And so I carried on to Hungerford, on through that spectacular red sandy country where big old boars, even from the air, are notoriously difficult to find. I mulled over what I had been told by both Richard Atkinson and, later, Keith Roberts: that while helicopter shoots had proven highly effective, and certainly more so than poison operations, feral pigs were still numerous and widespread back o' Bourke. Most of the stations here had professional hunters operating in them—two on Yantabulla, Keith said. They were from Bourke.

That the feral pig survives in such harsh country—actually fringing Australia's even more formidable hinterland—is largely, if not entirely, due to man. By bringing water from the earth to an otherwise dry land he made it possible to run sheep and cattle there but, at the same time, he made it equally suitable habitat for another of his domesticated animals that had cast aside all and any pretence of domesticity.

Presently I reached Hungerford, passing through a big iron gate and closing it behind me. It was just another section of the largest man-made fence in the world. The country on the Queensland side of the Dingo Fence looked exactly like it did on the New South Wales side of it. Funny that.

Back in its heyday of the 1870s–80s, Hungerford had three hotels, a school, and a population of about ninety people. Only the Royal Mail Hotel still stands and still functions in Hungerford today. Built in 1875, and in near original condition, it serves as a tangible reminder of a very different Australia: a time when Cobb & Co. stagecoaches and camel and bullock teams came this way, and when moleskin-clad drovers and stockmen in from the big stations tied their horses to the hitchrail outside the hotel and fronted up to the bar. I should imagine that a cold beer tasted as good then to a thirsty traveller as it does today in the cool public bar of the Royal Mail Hotel in Hungerford.

19 Game As They Come

Hammond Downs Station, On Cooper Creek, Southwest Queensland

Once again Joe Geiger's battered Toyota Landcruiser was making child's play of endless rock-like corrugations on the sun-hammered floodplains somewhere on the 28 328 hectare property he and his wife Nancy own.

As on the previous day, Joe, a warm-hearted soul, was taking enormous pleasure in showing me around their place and, in particular, some of the wildlife that shared the run with 5000 sheep and some 500 head of cattle. As Joe had explained, they would normally carry twice as many sheep as this but, because of a recent drought, they hadn't fully re-stocked.

'Maybe I'll catch a pig for you to photograph today,' Joe said matter-of-factly. A vivid mental picture of Joe mixing it with that big boar we had pursued yesterday sprang to mind.

'Like the boar we saw yesterday morning, Joe?' All very straight faced, of course.

'Now you're kidding! No, smaller than that.'

'Much smaller?'

'Bloody oath!'

I tapped the dashboard. 'You gonna catch it in this or on foot?'

'On foot!' Joe's eyebrows shot up in mock indignition. 'Hell, you reckon I'm buggered or something?'

I grinned at him. 'Didn't really pick you as a runner, Joe; that's all.'

'I can run if I have to.'

I was about to make an appropriate comment to that when Joe's words 'run down a pig' repeated themselves in my mind and a particularly unsettling experience, which had happened a matter of days before I visited Hammond Downs, dominated my thoughts.

In a similar situation to this, I had visited another station in southwest Queensland. The owner, clad in off-white moleskins and a grazier's flat-crowned hat, had, like Joe, taken me out to look over some of his considerable acres in a four-wheel-drive vehicle. Also along for the ride was the newly installed nanny, a slim and altogether lovely young European woman.

All went well until we saw pigs. They were resting under the one tree in sight at the time. Sensible. The temperature was about 45 degrees.

Previous to this sighting, my host had been, by turn, affable, charming, intelligent and even cultured. I'm sure he would have been far more at home in some European city than the young nanny was here on a sunbaked Queensland station.

Anyway, the pigs we had come across were all small ones; possibly they had lost their mother to professional shooters (on the place then) or 1080 poison (an extensive poison campaign was in progress—aimed directly at dingoes).

Upon spotting the pigs, an amazing transformation came over the station owner. Mouthing obscenities—no, snarling them—he gunned the vehicle and because the pigs had nowhere to hide on that broad grassy plain he systematically ran them down one after another, their crushed, broken bodies thump-thumping under the vehicle, a gut-wrenching sound. Cramped beside me, the nanny had turned quite pale and gave very indication, but thankfully didn't, of throwing up all over my lap.

With the last pig crunched up, the station owner's personality switched from an out-of- control Mr Hyde to a far more composed Dr Jekyll. It was, I suppose, all the more remarkable in the context of my visit to Hammond Downs: Joe Geiger genuinely cares for whatever wildlife—native or introduced—ranges their land. Joe in fact would no sooner run down a pig with a vehicle than he would a prize merino ram. Indeed, they do not let the RLPB use 1080 poison on

Left: Robert Martin, with Major, at Hay.

Below: Hungerford Gate, on the New South Wales section of the Dingo Fence (known locally as the 'Border Fence').

The Darling of all rivers near Wilcannia.

Sunset in the Snowy Mountains.

the place and I suspect that even if untold numbers of dingoes and pigs ever breached the nearby Dingo Fence—called the Barrier Fence locally—they would never use 1080 but, instead, would resort to the far more humane method of controlling animals with highpower rifles in the hands of skilled marksmen.

And presently—as he'd known he would—Joe spotted the kind of pig he intended to catch and have me photograph, although, to be truthful, what real use a shot of a grinning Joe holding a struggling pig would be presented something of a puzzle, but no matter.

So Joe roared after a bunch of maybe six or seven pigs and with a sudden sideways serve cut off a sow of around medium size.

'I thought you were going to do this on foot?' I said.

Joe merely smiled.

Within a few hundred metres the sow was starting to show signs of knocking up, and after half that distance again, she stopped. Joe stopped the vehicle then and started to run towards the sow which appeared to be breathing with some difficulty.

'That's cheating!' I called after him.

'Not around here it isn't!' he hurled back. 'C'mon, quit buggering around and get your camera.'

Smiling, I reached into the cabin and lifted my Nikon off the front seat; the 300 mm lens was attached to it in case the opportunity to photograph wildlife presented itself. Suddenly, Joe cried out and, spinning about, I saw the sow hurtling towards him. Instinctively, I aimed my camera at the action, and with no time to focus the lens correctly, triggered off a sequence of shots which really tell the story.

What happened was—and wasn't—funny.

It was hilarious in the sense that such an average-sized pig could barrel over a really big, heavy man such as Joe Geiger. But what wasn't amusing was that while Joe was flat on his back and trying to hold the aggressive sow at bay with his feet, she just might bite him.

Somehow, Joe, by squirming around, was able to grab hold of the sow's ears, and in that manner, he struggled to his rather shaky feet. He let the sow go then. She stood her ground, glaring at him. Carefully, Joe backed away until he considered it safe enough to turn his back on her.

'You hurt?' I asked, having great difficulty in hiding a smile.

'Bit bruised, I guess,' Joe said ruefully. 'Nothing broken, but.' He turned and looked back at the sow. She still stood there as though in the process of regaining her strength. Joe shook his head and the gesture was one of total admiration. And he said wth feeling, 'Game little bugger, isn't she?'

And that was it. The sow was game. As game as they come. But then that was really to be expected of her and the untold numbers of pigs that range Australia. The sow's distant ancestors were the type of animal that did not back down from wolves, that fought, and sometimes defeated, tigers. They also knew how to die with honour on the field of battle. The name of her species is a common one in many parts of the world. It is *Sus scrofa*.

20 South with the Paroo

I had a great deal of time to mull over things as I again drove through the big iron gate at Hungerford. Instead of retracing my steps to Bourke, I took the alternative route to Wilcannia via Wanaaring. The road more or less follows the course of the Paroo River and the Paroo is more often dry than not. Henry Lawson wrote a delightful poem about the Paroo River, in which was this line, ' "But where," said I, "is the blooming stream?" And he replied, "We're at it!" '

But there was plenty of red-tinged water in the Paroo today and the country was looking all the better for it.

Here in the Wanaaring Pastoral Protection Board, the feral pig situation is the same as it is in the Bourke, Milparinka, or Wilcannia districts—pretty much a serious problem for about 40 years. And the sheep stations I went by on that rutted red road—Talyeade, Glenhope and Moreland Downs—had all suffered extremely high lamb losses to rampaging pigs.

To provide such station people with practical advice on how best to combat agricultural and environmental damage caused by feral animals, the Bureau of Resource Sciences in 1993 published an information booklet entitled *Managing Vertebrate Pests: Principles and Strategies*. A segment under the heading 'Managing feral pig impact on lamb production. Optimising benefit and dealing with risk: a hypothetical example' is particularly in keeping with where I was somewhere north of Wanaaring in the broad channel of the Paroo River:

> Feral pig predation can cause an economically signifi-cant loss of winter lambs in western New South Wales. Several actions are available either alone or in combi-nation to reduce lamb predation Each has economic costs and associated risks. The manager's objective is to maximise benefit while taking appropriate account of associated risks. The following list of actions and risks is not exhaustive:
>
> • Poison or trap pigs in late summer to early autumn to reduce winter density:

Risks: pigs can be difficult to poison or trap outside winter, a few rogue boars that take the majority of lambs may not be removed and the manager may lack motivation before the problem becomes apparent.

• Coordinate lambing with neighbours to saturate predator and spread losses:

Risks: neighbours may not cooperate because feral pig distribution is patchy, and chance weather fluctuations may devastate all lamb production in a district.

• Change lambing to spring when alternative foods are available to pigs:

Risks: poorer lamb prices, and spring rainfall is less reliable, so more lambs may die or be stunted.

• Erect electric fence around lamb paddock:

Risks: fence may not exclude rogue boars, and a short-term break at a critical time could result in high loss of lambs.

• Only implement control when damage occurs:

Risks: losses may be unacceptable before action is taken and the range of control options is reduced.

Hypothetical or not, there appear to be a lot of sensible options presented here. But fencing does pose a problem inasfar as feral pigs are concerned. It is very much as Roma-based Jerry Stanley of the RLPB says: 'They don't care what sort of fence it is—even electric. If a pig wants to get through, it will.'

A case in point relating to electric fences happened on Peter Hall's station—The Mole—fringing the Macquarie Marshes in the mid-1970s. In sheer desperation, they strung up electric fencing to offer newly-born lambs some measure of protection from rampaging pigs that lived in the marshlands and struck at almost any time of the day or night. Audacity? You had to give them full marks for that. But electric fences would fix them good and proper, wouldn't they?

No they wouldn't!

The calcium-craving pigs, faced with soft-boned lambs, weren't about to let mere electric fences stop them. No way! So they could be seen on Hall's place running pellmell at the electric fencing, and, when they were close to it, as though preparing themselves mentally for what they now knew would happen, they would start screaming in anticipation of the electric hit.

So I thought about that aspect of a wild pig's behaviour and other aspects of their personalities and lifestyle I had heard or read about in the course of researching this book. I reflected, for instance, on the case of a well established population of wild pigs living at an altitude of 1000–2000 metres in the Snowy Mountains. High-ranging pigs indeed! They appeared to have a period of non-breeding in the summer and consequently did not have young in mid-winter. Along similar lines was a situation that developed in the southern Macquarie Marshes in late 1974/early 1975. Few if indeed any sows were found to be pregnant then, a time when following the floods of 1974 pig numbers were incredibly high and conditions were very dry. Quite simply there wasn't enough feed to go around as it was and Mother Nature, who moves in both marvellous and mysterious ways, acted accordingly so there wouldn't be more hungry mouths to feed. But then, we are talking about one of nature's great survivors, aren't we?

As Wanaaring drew close, I also thought about the hunting scene and the sheer numbers of men who hunted on a regular basis, and all those other people who, directly or indirectly, stood to gain because of it. And then there were the various Government departments working with feral pigs: the RLPB, the NPWS, the Department of Agriculture, the various town and city shires, there was almost no end to it. Again there were the graziers and fruit, cereal and vegetable growers who were troubled by feral pigs. It would in 1994 be enlightening to know precisely how many people throughout Australia are in one way or another affected by the feral pig. But whatever figure that may be—and a conservative guess says in the millions—then one thing stands out: there is no animal in Australia—native or introduced—that involves as many people as does the feral pig.

At Wanaaring I took time out for a tea break. Wanaaring? No, you wouldn't want to move from the big smoke to here. This is really back o' beyond territory, far, far beyond the proverbial black stump. Out here summer temperatures often climb to 50 degrees Celsius, blinding dust storms rage for days on end and for the most part the land is stricken with drought.

But today it wasn't too hot in Wanaaring, where a huge roadtrain was filling up with gas, and a couple of hard-looking types I picked as professional hunters were heading out of town in an open-backed vehicle with a teeth-like array of blood-encrusted hooks on either side. On second thoughts, maybe the professional hunters liked living in Wanaaring well enough.

On again. Just 256 kilometres of red sandy road to Wilcannia left now, a memorable visit to wild pig country fast coming to a close, and the Paroo that much closer to merging with the Darling of all rivers . . .

Appendix 1: A hunter's basic field care for the preparation and delivery of feral pigs for export meat purposes

- Dogs should not be used as this often causes extensive bruising of the animal which is prohibited for export game meat.
- Pigs must be shot in the head or neck, then immediately hung and bled. Slit the pig's throat for a minimum of 15 cm and remove that section of the windpipe. Stick the heart with a long-bladed knife through the opening just made to ensure positive bleeding.
- Animals are to be dressed within 15 minutes of killing.
- To dress out: remove the gut/anal passage without breakage. Gut spillage within the carcass will result in rejection. The brisket is not cut through. Testicles are removed from boars and udders from sows in milk or suckling. The chest diaphragm is cut across to allow drainage and cooling; the rest of the windpipe is removed. The lung, heart and liver are hung outside the chest still attached to the diaphragm; the kidneys are left in; the trotters, head and chest content remain intact.

- Vehicles must be clean and equipped with washing facilities (hands and knives are washed after each animal dressed out).
- Carcasses should remain hanging from when killed to delivery to allow airflow and reduce dust settlement on the inside tray or hanging rails of the vehicle.
- Carcasses not dressed out correctly or showing signs of disease or advanced emaciation will not be accepted.

The above must be regarded as a simple 'guideline' rather than a definitive set of rules. It pays to check current regulations and requirements relating to feral pigs for export before heading into the field. But generally speaking one is pretty safe if three basic rules are followed at all times: Keep them clean! Keep them fresh! Keep them hanging! And that, I guess, could very well be the motto of the feral pig export game trade.

Appendix 2: Recognised subspecies of *Sus scrofa* and where they are found

Sus scrofa subsp. *andamensis*   The Andam islands (a union territory of India); and, also two islands in the Bay of Bengal. Known as the Andaman wild pig.

Sus scrofa subsp. *assuricus*   Amur river region, northeast China.

Sus scrofa subsp. *attila*   The Caucasus Mountains and the Caspian Sea. Known as the Caucasian wild boar and renowned for its great size: fully grown males average 250–270 kg.

Sus scrofa subsp. *barbarus*   The western part of North Africa: Algeria, Tunisia and Morocco.

Sus scrofa subsp. *barbatus barbatus*   Borneo, the Malay Peninsular and Sumatra. Known as the Bormean wild or bearded pig.

Sus scrofa subsp. *castillanus*   Iberian peninsula.

Sus scrofa subsp. *celebenis*   Sulawesi (formerly the Celebes Islands); introduced to the island of Buru, east of Borneo.

Sus scrofa subsp. *chirodontus*   Many southeast Asian islands.

Sus scrofa subsp. *cristatus*   India, Pakistan, Burma and Sri Lanka. Known as the Indian crested pig/Asiatic wild boar.

Sus scrofa subsp. *floresianus*   Various southeast Asian islands.

Sus scrofa subsp. *koreanus*   Korea.

Sus scrofa subsp. *leucomystax*   Japan, that is, all Honshu region except northern parts.

Sus scrofa subsp. *libycus*   South Turkey, Palestine.

Sus scrofa subsp. *majori*   Italy.

Sus scrofa subsp. *meridionalis*   Sardinia.

Sus scrofa subsp. *moupinensis*   Central China, where two very distinct strains of this subspecies occur. Both are known as the Chinese wild pig.

Sus scrofa subsp. *nicobaricus*   Various Southeast Asian islands.

Sus scrofa subsp. *nigripes*   Central Asia, Mongolia, Afghanistan.

Sus scrofa subsp. *papuensis*   Papua New Guinea; adjacent islands.

Sus scrofa subsp. *philippenis*   Various islands in the Philippine group.

Sus scrofa subsp. *reiseri*   Former Yugoslavia.

Sus scrofa subsp. *riukivanus*   A number of islands in Japanese waters—that is, not on the mainland.

Sus scrofa subsp. *salvanis*   Nepal, Sikkim and Bhutan. Known as the pygmy hog (a fully grown adult will reach no more than 30 centimetres at the shoulder). Not seen for many years and possibly now extinct.

Sus scrofa subsp. *scrofa*   Middle and western Europe, eastern parts of the former USSR; North Africa.

Sus scrofa subsp. *timorensis*   Various Southeast Asian islands, including Timor.

Sus scrofa subsp. *verrocus*   Java, Papua New Guinea, the lesser Sundra and Maluku islands.

Sus scrofa subsp. *vittatus*   Malay Archipelago; Sumatra, Java; other islands.

Sus scrofa subsp. *timorensis* is the most likely subspecies to have first ranged in a feral situation in Australia.

Appendix 3: Close relatives of *Sus scrofa*

Red river hog *Potamochoerus porcus porcus*
Considered a subspecies of bush pig, this is perhaps the most striking of all wild pigs. Found mostly near water (it is an excellent swimmer), the red river hog is a medium-sized pig, bright orange-red in colour with distinctive black and white markings on the face, long tufts of white on the ends of the ears, a white crest along the spine, and a long tail. In old age males may turn black.

Red river hogs often force tunnels through heavy undergrowth and, using their shoulders and backs, lever up interlocked vegetation to form effective roofs over their dens. Like other pigs they are gregarious, living in groups of up to twenty. Older boars, however, may decide to live in isolation. The range of the red river hog is western Africa, particularly Equatorial Guinea; close relatives are found in Cameroon, Liberia and Congo.

South African bush pig *Potamochoerus porcus koiropotamus*
Standing in excess of 76 cm at the shoulder, and weighing up to 90 kg, the bush pig is covered with coarse hair, most males being blackish-brown, with females tending more to brown intermixed with grey.

Like other pigs, they are omnivorous, but given the choice they seem to prefer vegetation. A farmer's crops are always in favour where the bush pig is concerned and, under cover of night, they gain access to maize or potato crops by burrowing under fences or, if that is not possible, by snapping the wires. Not even a barbed-wire fence will stop a determined bush pig.

The range is southeastern Africa. A smaller but very similar cousin, the Madagascar bush pig (*Potamochoerus porcus larvatus*) is found only on the island of Madagascar, where, in the north, it poses a continual threat to the gravely endangered Malagasy tortoise.

Forest hog *Hyloehoerus meinertzhageni*
This is the largest of African pigs and it is a big animal by any standards, standing up to 1 metre at the shoulder and weighing up to 230 kg. Generally speaking, the forest hog is a heavy-set, blackish-grey pig with a somewhat scanty coat of stiff hairs (the skin may show through the hairs) It has a heavy wart below the eye and a distinct tuft at the end of a long tail; it bears a marked resemblance to the much better-known warthog of the African plains, which is its nearest relative.

Like the red river hog, it tunnels extensively in dense underbrush, creating linking pathways that lead to huge communal dens occupied by families for generations. Unlike the red river hog, however, it seldom digs or roots, but feeds on leaves, grasses and, should the opportunity arise, small birds and mammals.

The male forest hog is known for his aggressive nature, especially when protecting his territory or his family. He may charge without warning and that might prove fatal, for he may grow tusks that protrude from his lower jaw for a good 23 cm.

The forest hog can be found in high-altitude forests, as a rule, from Kenya and Tanzania through Congo to Cameroon.

Warthog *Phacochoerus aethiopicus*
Easily the most recognisable of the African pigs (because of the number of times it has been featured on television), the warthog derives its name from two very prominent warts on either side of its face. An adult may reach 86 cm at the shoulder, have a length of 1.5 metres and weigh 150 kg. The normal colour is a blackish-grey; like the forest hog, it is sparsely covered with bristly hairs, so the skin is exposed. A heavy mane extends down the back and on either side of the body. The tail is well tufted. Oddly enough, the young, in contrast with other pigs, are not striped at birth.

While some consider the warthog an ugly and ferocious-looking customer, the truth is that they are by nature rather friendly souls, forming lasting family attachments. Living on the hot plains means they have many natural enemies, such as lions, cheetahs and leopards. Because of this they have been given the most impressive fighting weapons of any member of the pig family. Record tusks may measure 60 cm, but a more normal set will be around 25–30 cm.

Most predators, with a plump young warthog in mind for supper, think twice before committing themselves to attack. They know that the young are almost always under strict control, close to a watchful adult. A sudden charge to take an unsuspecting young warthog will result, almost certainly, in a reaction of untold fury. Of course, many young and adult warthogs are taken by carnivores—especially by lions operating in packs—but they are often able to drive away a cheetah or leopard or even a lion operating on its own. Pound for pound there is no animal on the African continent that can fight so fiercely and so

effectively. The same trait is, of course, alive in the wild boar wherever it is found.

Babirusa *Babirusa babirusa*
There are apparently two forms of this medium-to-large pig, one found on the large island of Sulawesi (formerly called Celebes) and the other on the island known as Togian. The former (*B. b. celebensis*) is almost bald, its creased skin slate grey. The latter is sparsely covered with greyish hair. Either way, the males grow extremely large tusks, second in size only to those of the warthog.

The babirusa is a real puzzle. It has, for instance, two stomachs; and like a cow chews its cud. Indeed, its Malay name suggests something enigmatic: *babi* means pig, *rusa* means deer. In its dense rainforest habitat the babirusa eats like a sheep, runs like a deer, and can swim like a champion.

Today the babirusa is possibly endangered, the main reason being that tribesmen believe that its tusks hold special magic powers. The flesh of this pig is considered a delicacy (a report in a United States Agency for International Development publication in 1985 said the babirusa might be a kosher pig whose meat could be eaten by Jews and Muslims). Despite the fact that the Indonesian government has placed the babirusa on the protected list, hunting still goes on. In 1986 a team of zoologists was unable to find any traces of the babirusa in Sulawesi's deep rainforests. Prior to the 1970s the babirusa roamed here freely in large numbers. The babirusa has been liberated on the island of Buru, east of Sulawesi.

Peccary *Tayassus tajacu*
Also known as javelina or musk pig, peccaries differ from true pigs for a number of reasons and have been separated into a special family, Tayassuidae. Differences include their upper, dagger-like tusks, which are directed straight downwards rather than upwards and outwards, their one lateral hoof (or dew-claw) on each hind leg, and their small, raised, practically functionless lateral hooves. Also, they have a large musk gland on the back, about 20 cm from the tail. Like the babirusa's, the peccary's litter rarely exceeds two.

While various forms of peccary exist, there are two main types. Generally speaking, they are sturdy, compact animals standing up to 63 cm at the shoulder and weighing around 30 kg. The collared peccary, which is found from the southwest of the USA through to Patagonia, is tawny and black, appearing grizzled or speckled, with a light grey collar and white lip or chin. In Costa Rica, the collared peccary has a tawny, instead of lighter, collar. The white-lipped peccary, found from Mexico to Paraguay, is less tawny and more black, and is slightly larger. Lesser forms are found in the low forested region of Honduras, in northwestern Mexico, and in Paraguay and northern Argentina.

Appendix 4: Address list: locations of professional hunting guides and stations offering pig hunting

Outfitter	*Proprietor*	*Address/phone*	*Hunt location*
New South Wales			
Bruce Sharpe Safaris	Bruce Sharpe	'Comeroo', Bourke NSW 2840 Ph: (068) 74 7735	Northwest NSW
Coolabah Farm Holidays	Keith and Mari Norris	'Boorara' Coolabah NSW 2831 Ph: (086) 33 2174	Coolabah NSW
Goonoo Safaris	Adam Curry	21 Quinn Street, Dubbo NSW 2830 Ph (068) 828 469	Throughout Australia
Hunt Australia	Bob and Kay Penfold	72 Blanch Street, Shortland NSW 2307 Ph: (049) 51 1198	Vic, Qld
Inland Australia	John Abbott	PO Box 19, Girilambone NSW 2831 Ph: (068) 33 1022	Central NSW
M.J. & G.J. Johnson	Mervyn Johnson	'Pendiana', Coolabah NSW 2831 Ph: (068) 332 183	Western NSW
Mullagalah Safaris	Max Smith	8 Bareena Drive, Balgowlah Heights NSW 2093 Ph: (02) 948 8449	Western NSW
Narran River Safaris	Martin Maxwell	'Tucki', New Angledool NSW 2832 Ph: (068) 29 0393	Northwestern NSW and southwest Qld
Rocky Safaris	Russell Stewart	PO Box 144, Narrabri NSW 2390 Ph: (067) 92 2878	Australia
Scrub Holidays	Carmine Cantone	PO Box 548, Cobar NSW 2835 Ph: (068) 363 225	Western NSW
The Ridges	Richard and Toni Ridge	'Wancobra', Bourke NSW 2840 Ph: (068) 747 604	Western NSW
W. & M. Mitchell	Wal Miitchell	'Lansdown', Louth NSW 2840 Ph: (068) 747 443	Western NSW
Wilderness Hunting Adventures	John and Di Hall	Nyngan NSW Ph: (068) 33 2178	Nyngan and Coolabah regions
Queensland			
Air Cairns	Vic Mail	PO Box 129, Stratford Qld 4870 Ph: (070) 35 9003	Cape York
Bob Fisher	Bob Fisher	164 Scarborough Street, Southport Qld 4215 Ph: (075) 32 0024	Qld, NT, New Caledonia
Central Queensland Safaris	Gary and Robyn Cory	15 Hilder Street. Loganholme Qld 4129 Ph: (07) 209 9591	Western Qld
Ghost Gum Safaris	Lionel Mundt	PO Box 66, Beenleigh Qld 4207 Ph: (07) 807 2244	Qld, NSW, NT, Africa, British Columbia
Guided Hunting and Fishing Safaris	Bud and Vic Quaid	PO Box 349, Mossman Qld 4873 Ph: Bud (070) 98 8264, Vic (070) 359 003	Top End of Qld

Outfitter	*Proprietor*	*Adress/phone*	*Hunt location*
Havago Hunting	Jim Dieckmann	'Nyora', Millmerran Qld 4357 Ph: (076) 67 4152	Qld, NT
International and Australian Hunting Safaris	Chis Kahler	30 Cockleshell Court, Runaway Island Qld 4216 Ph: (075) 37 5105	Australia
Maranoa Safaris	Alan Moon	PO Box 442, St George Qld 4487 Ph: (076) 25 3884	Western Qld
Muckadilla Hunting Safaris	Glenn Giffin	91 Stephen Street, Camp Hill Qld 4152 Ph: (07) 398 2082	Qld
Niall Safaris	Mick and Maisie Anning	'Niall', Charters Towers Qld 4820 Ph: (077) 70 4461	Charters Towers
Ostende	Adrian Cooney	PO Box 201, Woolloongabba Qld 4102 Ph: (07) 848 6198	Southwest Qld
Western Weekenda	Andy Cameron	'Argyll', Morben Qld 4468 Ph: (076) 54 8230	Western Qld
World Wide Hunts	Rick Nagle	932 Kinka Beach, M/S 1626, Yeppoon Qld 4703 Ph: (079) 39 6437	Australia

Victoria

Australian South Pacific Safaris	Kevin McCormick	Fentondale RSD, Clarkefield Vic 3430 Ph: (054) 28 5372	Australia
Bar W Trail Rides & Outfitters	Neville and Lyn Wright	RMB 1800, Moyhu Vic 3732 Ph: (057) 29 7536	Northeast Vic
Blackstump Safaris	Myrone Girdler	PO Box Toongabbie Vic 3856 Ph: (051) 92 4470	Woonnagatta Station, Vic, southern Qld, northern NSW
Maverick Safaris	Alan and Patricia White	PO Box 253, Ashburton Vic 3147 Ph/Fax: (03) 885 2935	Australia
Murray Thomas Safaris	Murray Thomas	5 Tabor Court, Sunbury Vic 3429 Ph: (03) 774 7852	Australia
R & S Safaris	Robert Black	20 Lawrence Crescent, Noble Park Vic 3174 Ph: (03) 885 2935	NSW and NT
Southern Safaris	John Steer	PO Box 14, Daylesford Vic 3460 Ph: (053) 478 556 Fax: (053) 478 731	Vic and NT

South Australia

Outback Horizons Adventure Holidays	Bexley Carman	PO Box 84, Alberton SA 5014 Ph: (08) 47 7711	Western NSW

Western Australia

Kalbarri Pig Shooting Safaris	Lindsay Edwards	PO Box 113, Kalbarri WA 6536 Ph: (099) 371 393	WA
Wagoe Ridge Farm	Barry Burgess	PO Box 65, Kalbarri WA 6536 Ph: (099) 37 1003	WA

Northern Territory

Arafura Safaris	Simon and Scott Kyle-Little	PO Box 40813, Casuarina NT 0811 Ph: (089) 27 2372	Southeast Arnhem Land
Davidson Safaris	Max and Philippa Davidson	PO Box 41905. Casuarina NT 0811 Ph: (089) 27 5240, Fax: (089) 450 919	Arnhem Land, Cobourg Peninsula
Northern Territory Outback Safaris	Rob and Kay Penfold	72 Blanch Street, Shortland NSW 2307 Ph: (049) 51 1198	NT
Safaris North	Steve and Niki Fullerton	PO Box 1859, Katherine NT 0851 Ph: (089) 72 3089	Arnhem Land
Wimray Safaris	Ray Allwright	PO Box 1634, Darwin NT 0801 Ph: (089) 452 755	Arnhem Land, Cobourg Peninsula

Appendix 5: Trophy hunting

A boar's tusks are a true miracle of nature. Protruding wickedly from his lower jaw, they are obviously fighting, not digging, tools. Tusks are sharpened by grinding or rubbing them against the small, upper tusks which are called grinders. The act of sharpening also prevents the bottom tusks from growing too long and becoming useless as offensive or defensive weapons.

Should a boar lose a grinder, or even both of them, his tusk or tusks will grow unchecked. If the lower tusks fail to fit into the correct position behind the grinders when the mouth is closed, the same thing will happen. Such tusks have been known to pass right through the cheek and to re-enter the jawbone. What pain this causes a boar we can only speculate, but we can take it for granted it wouldn't make his disposition any sweeter. Still growing, the tusk will finally pass right through the jawbone and enter the tongue channel inside the boar's mouth. Such a tusk, which is no longer sharpened or restricted from growing, is called a 'bracelet' tusk, for obvious reasons.

As a matter of interest, natives in Timor and Papua New Guinea have a particularly gruesome habit. They catch young boars and knock out their grinders. Later, when the boar is recaptured, the resultant ivory is removed for chest decorations. Many tusks of this type have been known to measure 45 cm overall— that is, from their base to their rounded, blunted tip. One highly prized set reached a staggering 66 cm.

On those extremely rare occasions when a boar of great age is killed it is common to find his tusks have long since ceased growing. For instance, the grinders may have rotted away and the lower tusks, although showing signs of their former grind length at the base of grinding, are now more rounded at the edges where they were once sharp.Such tusks are still quite sharp at their points and are usually polished on their edges or lips to a high, varnish-like finish.

The Douglas Score

In scoring tusks by the Douglas Score method, a drawn set of tusks can only qualify is they have been normally and naturally ground by the top tusks of the boar, and, by that criterium, the bracelet type of tusk does not qualify. From the diagram below and the Douglas score card for my Arnhem Land trophy on page130 we see how a boar's tusks are measured and scored.

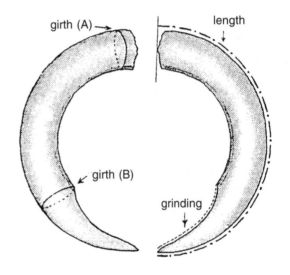

Measurements taken:

The measurements taken are illustrated on the score card. They are:

1. Length on outside curve.
2. Girth at the base of the tusk.
3. Girth at the base of grinding.
4. Length of the grinding.

All these measurements are taken to the nearest eighth of an inch; a fabric tape may be used if it has first been found correct by a test with a steel one.

Extracted Pig Tusks
(DOUGLAS SCORE)

OWNER. . . . .

KILLED BY .PHILIP .HOLDEN . . . .

LOCALITY & DATE EAST. ALLIGATOR .RIVER.,
. . . ARNHEM .LAND,. JULY .1993. . . . .

Steel Tape Measurements of	Left	Right	Score *Shorter measurement dbld.*
LENGTH	7²/₈	7²/₈	14⁴/₈
Girth at Base of Tusk (A)	2²/₈	2²/₈	4⁴/₈
Girth at Base of Grinding (B)	2²/₈	2¹/₈	4²/₈
Length of Grinding	2	2	4
TOTAL SCORE		27²/₈	

*A fabric tape may be used if it has first been found correct by test with a steel one.

The SCI method of measuring pig tusks

A. *Length of Tusk*

Measure the length of each tusk on its outer curve, from the farthest point on the base, to the tip. Because the base, or root end, of the tusk is characteristically jagged, its farthest point may not be on the line of measurement. If not 'card' it off with a straight edge held at a right angle to the axis of the tusk and begin where the straight edge intersects the line of measurement. If the tip of the tusk is broken, card it off in the same manner. Do not measure across the flat end of a broken tusk.

B. *Circumference of tusk*

Measure the circumference of each tusk at its largest place, which will normally be at the gumline. Use a light tape at a right angle to the axis of the tusk.

When measuring circumferences of very small tusks such as those of water deer, a more accurate measurement can often be obtained with a cloth or plastic sewing tape or by wrapping a piece of paper around the tusk and marking the points of intersection. This is an excepton to the normal rule requiring a steel tape or cable.

C. *Total score*

Total all measurements. Record fractions in 1/8ths of an inch.

When the base of a tusk is filled with plaster or other taxidermic material, be careful to measure only the actual tusk—do not measure taxidermic material. When a tusk cannot be removed from a mounted head only the measurable part that is outside the head may be recorded. Do not estimate or allow for tusk material that is inside the mount.

By following these instructions, we can see how my same Arnhem Land trophy fared:

	Left	*Right*
A. Length of tusk	7²/₈	7²/₈
B. Circumference of tusk	2²/₈	2²/₈
C. Total score	19⁶/₈	

For the record, the highest scoring South Pacific wild boar is credited to Noel J. Brown of Queensland:

	Left	*Right*
Length of tusk	9⁴/₈	10²/₈
Circumference of tusk	2³/₈	2⁴/₈
Score	24⁵/₈	

Appendix 6: Current legislation and the structure of pest management (feral pig)

Primary responsibility for feral pig management lies with landowners and occupiers, whether government or non-government. Each State and Territory, as well as the Commonwealth, has its own structural arrangement and suite of legislation to regulate vertebrate pest management within its respective jurisdiction.

Australian Capital Territory
The principal act in the Australian Capital Territory is the *Rabbit Destruction Act 1919*. The ACT Parks and Conservation Service of the Department of Environment, Land and Planning has primary responsibility for vertebrate pest management in the national park and nature reserves that represent approximately 40 per cent of the ACT. The Service provides advice and assistance on vertebrate pest control to rural lessees, although rural land is now a relatively small proportion of the ACT.

New South Wales
The *Rural Lands Protection Act 1989* is the principal act regulating vertebrate pest management. It establishes the 57 autonomous Rural Lands Protection Boards which have primary responsibility for ensuring vertebrate pest management within their respective areas. The RLPBs report to the minister responsible for agriculture and rural affairs.

Queensland
The *Rural Lands Protection Act 1985–1990* provides the principal powers for regulating vertebrate pest management. The Land Protection Branch of the Department of Lands is the primary vertebrate pest management agency.

Northern Territory
The *Territory Parks and Wildlife Conservation Act 1988* is the principal act used to manage vertebrate pests. Vertebrate pest policy development and control is coordinated jointly by the Conservation Commission and the Department of Primary Industry and Fisheries. Pests or pest areas can be declared under this Act, which also has provisions to require control to be undertaken.

Western Australia
The Agriculture Protection Board is constituted under the *Agriculture Protection Board Act 1950*. Administration of the Agriculture and Related Resources Protection Act 1976, which is the principal Act for vertebrate pest and weed management, is delegated to the APB.

Victoria
The *Vermin and Noxious Weeds Act 1958* provides the principal powers for regulating vertebrate pests. It is administered by the Land and Catchment Protection Branch of the Department of Conservation and Natural Resources. The Department was formed by the amalgamation of former conservation, forest and land departments and elements of environment, planning and water resources departments. The aim was to bring together in one department all sections responsible for land and water resource management.

Appendix 7: Member organisations of the Vertebrate Pests Committee and contacts for information regarding feral pigs

Executive Officer
Wildlife Division
Conservation Commission of the
Northern Territory
PO Box 496
Palmerston NT 0831

Chief
Animal & Plant Control
Commission
GPO Box 1671
Adelaide SA 5001

Unit Manager
Vertebrate Pests Land & Catchment
Protection Branch
Department of Conservation &
Natural Resources
250 Victoria Parade
Melbourne VIC 3000

Chief
Division of Wildlife & Ecology
CSIRO
PO Box 84
Lyneham ACT 2602

The Director
Agricultural Production & Natural
Resources Branch
Bureau of Resource Sciences
GPO Box E11
Queen Victoria Terrace
Parkes ACT 2600

Manager
Wildlife Research Unit
ACT Parks & Conservation Service
PO Box 1119
Tuggeranong ACT 2901

Director
Wildlife Management Unit
Australian National Parks & Wildlife
Service
PO Box 636
Canberra City ACT 2601

Executive Director
Rural Lands Protection Board
PO Box 168
North Quay QLD 4002

Manager
Agricultural Production
NSW Agriculture
Locked Bag 21
Orange NSW 2800

Chief Executive Officer
Agricultural Protection Board
Baron-Hay Court
South Perth WA 6151

Appendix 8: Taxidermist address list

Name	Propietor	Address/Telephone
Mel Burton Taxidermy	Mel Burton	Woodford Road, Kilcoy Qld 4515 Ph: (074) 971 486
Mick Doellinger Taxidermy	Mick Doellinger	3 Jensen Street. Aratula Qld 4309 Ph: (074) 63 8322
North American Taxidermy Specialists	Tony Psaila	163 William Street, St Albans Vic 3021 Ph: (03) 366 2490
North Western Taxidermy Studio	Joe Gajdos	16 Dandarbong Avenue, Carlingford NSW 2118 Ph: (02) 874 1502
Otto Ruf Taxidermy	Otto Ruf	9 Frances Street, Greensborough Vic 3038
Red Wing Taxidermy	George Pisani	Londonderry NSW 2753 Ph: (047) 77 4980
Robinson's Taxidermy	George Robinson	Mail Service 292, Blacksoil Qld 4306 Ph: (07) 264 1566
Tantune	Sammy Furnari	Ingleburn NSW 2565 Ph: (02) 605 4788
Universal Taxidermy Studios	Robert Jakovejevic	16 Mowle Street, Westmead NSW 2145 Ph: (02) 633 4294

Selected Reading

Books

Australian Places. Reader's Digest, Australia, first edition.

Baden-Powell, R. *Pig-Sticking, or Hog-Hunting.* H. Jenkins, London, 1924.

Brander, M. (editor). *The International Encyclopedia of Shooting.* Pelham Books, London, 1972.

Captain Cook in Australia. (Edited by A.W. Reed.) Reed, Wellington, 1969.

Complete Book of Australian Mammals. Angus & Robertson, 1983.

Conquest, R.H. *The Spurs Are Rusty Now.* Ure Smith, Sydney, 1963.

Darwin, C.L. *The Variation of Animals and Plants Under Domestication.* John Murray, London, 1868.

Dahl, K. *In Savage Australia.* Philip Allan & Co. Ltd. London, 1926.

Douglas, N. *The Douglas Score.* NZDA publication, Wellington, 1959.

Hamerton, P.G. *Chapters on Animals.* Robert Bros, Boston, Mass., 1884

Heptner, V.G.; Naumov, N.P., Bannikov, A.C. *Die Saugetiere der Sowjetunion.* VEB Gustav Fischer Verlag, Jena, 1966.

Hill, E. *The Territory.* Angus & Robertson, 1951.

Lever, C. *Naturalised Mammals of the World.* Longman Group Inc., New York, 1985.

MacLean, A. *Captain Cook.* Collins, London, 1972.

Mellen, I. *The Natural History of the Pig.* Exposition Press, New York, 1953.

Pike, G. *Wings Over The Cape.* Pinevale Publications, for Cape York Air Services, Cairns (undated).

Rappaport, R.A. *Pigs For The Ancestors.* Yale University Press, New Haven, 1968.

Reader's Digest Book of Facts. Reader's Digest, Australia, 1968.

Reed, A.H., and Reed A.W. *Captain Cook in New Zealand.* Reed, Wellington, 1951.

Reid, J.W. *Pigs.* Farmers & Stock-breeders Publications Limited, London, 1955.

Rolls, E.C. *They All Ran Wild.* Angus & Robertson Ltd, Sydney, 1969.

Scenic Wonders of Australia. Reader's Digest, Australia, 1976.

Singe, J. *The Torres Strait: People and History.* University of Queensland Press, 1989.

Stokes, J.L. *Discoveries in Australia.* T. & W. Boone, London, 1846.

Tisdell, C.A. *Wild Pigs: Environmental Pest or Economic Resource?* Pergamon Press, Australia, 1982.

Webb, G., and Manolis, C. *Crocodiles of Australia.* Reed, Australia, 1989.

Other sources

Caley, P. *The Ecology and Management of Feral Pigs in the 'Wet-Dry' Tropics of the Northern Territory* (final report to the Conservation Commission on the Douglas–Daly feral pig study), 1993.

'Council declares war on feral pigs.' *Northern Beachcomber,* 2 July 1993.

Cutler, R.S. 'An overview of the pig industry'. *Aust. Vet.* 66, 429-31. 1989.

Feral Animals. Public Forum Papers (Nature Resources Conservation League of Victoria), Bairnsdale 4–5 April 1981.

Feral Pigs and Their Distribution. Information bulletin, RLPB, 1987.

Feral Pigs in New South Wales. Aust. Meat Research Committee Review, 1978.

Flynn, D.M. *Report on vertebrate pests and exotic animal diseases.* Aust. Bureau of Animal Health, Canberra.

Hallack, E.H. *Kangaroo Island: Adelaide's Sanatorium.* W.K. Thomas, Adelaide, 1905.

Hone, J. 'How Many Feral Pigs in Australia?' *Aust. Wildl. Res.,* 1990.

Hone, J., and Atkinson, B. 'Evaluation of fencing to control feral pig movements.' *Aust. Wildl. Res.* 10, 499-505, 1983.

Hone, J., and Robarbs, G.E. 'Feral Pigs: Ecology and Control.' *Wool Tech. Sheep Breed.,* 1980.

Hone, J., and Waithman, J. 'Feral Pigs are spreading'. *Agric. Gazette of NSW,* Vol. 90, No. 2, 1979.

Korn, T. *Control of Feral Pigs in the Macquarie Marshes.* Dept. of NSW.

'Man's best friend a pig?' *Sunday Territorian,* 8 November 1985.

McKnight, T. *Friendly Vermin: a survey of feral livestock in Australia.* University of California Publication in Geography, 1976.

McIlroy, J.C.; Braysher, M., and Saunders, G.R. *Effectiveness of a warfarin-poisoning campaign against feral pigs in Namadgi National Park, ACT* Australian Wildlife Research 16, 195–202, 1989.

McIlroy, J.C., and Saillard, R.J. *The effect of hunting with dogs on the numbers and movements of feral pigs and subsequent success of poisoning exercises in Namadgi National Park.* ACT Australian Wildlife Research 16, 353–363, 1989.

O'Brian, P. *Managing Introduced Pests.* Resource Sciences Interface No. One (undated).

'"Piggy" swaps the lab for adventure.' *The Wet Tropics Newspaper*, Issue No. 1. Wet Season 1993.

'Private life of the wild pig.' *Journal of Agriculture*, No. 3, WA, 1981.

Pullar, E.M. 'The wild (feral) pigs of Australia and their role in the spread of infectious disease.' *Australian Vet. Journal* 26: 99–110, 1950.

Safari Club International entry form, for method of scoring pig tusks.

'Safari Directory.' *Sporting Shooter*, February 1993.

'Taxidermy Guide', *Sporting Shooter*, March 1993.

The Cassowary in Queensland. Wildlife Information. NPWS, 1990.

The ecology of feral pigs. Information bulletin. RLPB, undated.

Townsend, S.E. 'Some notes on feral pigs and their distribution in Victoria.' *Vic. Nat.* Vol. 98. January/February 1981.

'Wild pig attacks camper.' *Northern Territory News*, 1 November 1988.

Index